Praise for *Getting My Hands Dirty*

"Chuck Hutchison embodies all that Coach Woody Hayes sought to teach to his Buckeye team at The Ohio State University. Chuck is a terrific model of what it takes to reach your full potential in all that you do. Mastering his fundamentals of curiosity, confidence, and conviction, Chuck excelled in every endeavor. Dig in and learn from a winner!"

—Jim Tressel, Ohio lieutenant governor; president emeritus of Youngstown State University; and former head football coach at The Ohio State University and Youngstown State University

"A powerful memoir that will appeal to more than just football fans. An inspirational read that is attractive, enlightening, and a beacon of hope for personal change and those envisioning a better future."

—Midwest Book Review

"A memoir about transformation. It's not just about football, or gardening, or even family—it's about the courage to begin again, no matter how many times life knocks you down."

—Manhattan Book Review

"A heartfelt memoir from an ex-football player, *Getting My Hands Dirty* is about sports, business, and the healing, meditative power of gardening. Earnest and entertaining."

—*Foreword* Clarion Reviews

"Hutchinson's wry observations and laugh-out-loud humor contain powerful lessons about the simple (but not always easy) rules that lead to success, despite hurdles and heartbreak. Yes, you have to do the work, and yes, you may have to get your hands dirty along the way. As Hutchinson's account makes clear, however, the rewards can be immense."

—Gail Harris, creator and host of the PBS series *Body & Soul;* author of *Body & Soul: Your Guide to Health, Happiness, and Total Well-Being,* and *Finders Seekers*

Getting My Hands Dirty

Getting My Hands Dirty

A MEMOIR OF RESILIENCE AND TRANSFORMATION
FROM THE GRIDIRON TO THE GARDEN

Chuck Hutchison

GFB

Published by GFB™, Seattle
www.girlfridayproductions.com

Produced by Girl Friday Productions

Cover design: Lauren Smith
Production editorial: Kylee Hayes
Project management: Sara Spees Addicott

Image credits: cover © Shutterstock/Derek Hatfield

ISBN (paperback): 978-1-967510-04-7
ISBN (ebook): 978-1-967510-05-4

Library of Congress Control Number: 2025911607

First edition

Contents

Preface

"Gentlemen, you are passing through here on your way to somewhere else." Those were the foremost words I heard from my first head coach in professional football. I didn't know it at the time, but his message of uncertainty and change would apply throughout my entire life: through my early years learning the lessons of hard work on a dairy farm in Ohio, to becoming a Buckeye and playing on a championship team under legendary football coach Woody Hayes, to a too-short career in the NFL, to building and coaching a team in the erstwhile United States Football League, and to working my way from the bottom of one of the nation's leading food manufacturers to the top, serving one of the world's biggest brands.

Along the way, I navigated life as a father and a husband—a journey full of both boundless love and heartbreaking struggle.

But none of these experiences prepared me for what I was to encounter in my retirement. In many ways, my life to that point had prepared the field, and it was up to me to grow something beautiful from my pain.

"You should write a book!" Well-meaning friends have made this suggestion many times over the past decade. Having heard many of my life's stories, they thought my perspectives and the lessons I've learned would be of interest to others. There's just one problem: I am not much of a reader. Growing up, I read a few books on sports, but it was mostly to pass the time before I fell asleep. Otherwise, I was working on the farm or out playing football or baseball instead of just reading about them.

I decided that if I was going to take on such an ambitious project as creating a chronicle of my life, then it needed to be about more than just telling stories. It would also be about the takeaways. About the things that molded and shaped me, that helped me get where I got and learn what I learned.

This book is meant to provide more than just entertainment—a way to pass the time until *you* fall asleep. Though if I've done my job well, there will be plenty of entertainment, too. My greatest hope is that you'll walk away from reading my stories feeling changed in some way. That there will be at least one kernel of wisdom—maybe more, if we're lucky—that shifts the way you see the world, or *your* world, and that inspires you and helps you connect with your internal motivation or see a clearer path through a difficult situation. If that happens, then for me, this exercise will have been well worth it.

But if it doesn't, truth be told, it will still have been worth it. This project, which I embarked on thinking it might end up as little more than a memory book for my grandkids and which has now taken me several years to accomplish, has provided me something I never expected. Looking back on my life as a journey and considering what I learned along the way, reflecting on the many pivotal moments, has helped me see that there was a blueprint for everything I have experienced.

As you read these pages, my wish and blessing for you is that in peering behind the curtain of my life, your own blueprint will start to become clear.

—Chuck Hutchison
Asheville, North Carolina, February 2025

Part One

CHAPTER 1

Do Your Best

There is something that happens to the human brain when you have an abundance of options. It's not a good thing. To some extent, we know that. I mean, who hasn't stood in the cereal aisle or scrolled through an online store and been dumbfounded by the sheer volume of possibilities? According to psychologists, having an excess of options isn't just overwhelming, it can also make us less happy. Scientists call it the paradox of choice.

So, I guess I should thank my parents for the fact that during my first seventeen years on this planet, life offered few options. What choices did present themselves were largely made either for me or by the paucity of my surroundings.

I was raised in Malvern, Ohio, a rural town in northeastern Ohio. Employment opportunities consisted of farming, factory work, and mining. Of the eighty-eight counties in the state, ours was one of the poorest. To put it into perspective, Carroll County was one of the first areas to receive federal funding to improve reading and writing skills.

The town square consisted of a café, a drugstore, a grocery, a bank, a funeral home, a hardware store, a beauty parlor, a barbershop, and an equal number of bars and churches: five. Consistent with the town's offerings, educational opportunities were limited. There were two high schools in the county, Malvern and Carrollton. Malvern was the smallest, with an enrollment of fewer than one hundred compared to Carrollton's nearly one thousand.

My first-grade class was composed of twenty-four students, all of whom remained together through high school. By the time we were seniors, we were more like family than classmates. As we got older, no one dated each other—it would have felt incestuous. Our class officers were the same students every year, and the smartest and most popular classmates remained so until graduation.

Teachers were lifers. Many of my teachers had taught my dad the very same subjects I was learning. It's one thing for teachers to compare your learning progress to that of your older siblings, but to be compared to your dad is a little creepy. The school's facilities and equipment were on par with the deteriorating condition of the buildings. One building housed grades one through eight and the second was for nine through twelve.

Sports teams consisted of varsity football, basketball, and baseball. Extracurricular offerings were cheerleading, band, choir, and the chess club. Girls were cheerleaders and in the choir. The boys who were physically able played sports and the rest were in the band. Educational and sports offerings were commensurate with our school's size and fiscal means. Latin was the only foreign language on offer, and biology was taught without the benefit of microscopes. (I'll let you picture that for a moment.)

The high school gymnasium was so cramped that to play basketball was to take your well-being into your own hands.

Anyone driving for a layup had to first make the shot, then quickly brace for the ensuing collision with the gymnasium wall. It paid to develop your three-pointer, but only if the arc was low. The ceiling height required the lights be enclosed in cages to prevent them from shattering.

Our football equipment, on the other hand, was purchased secondhand from bigger schools that could afford new equipment and uniforms. If you were a starting player, your equipment was sized properly and you looked the part of an athlete. The reserves wore whatever remained and hoped for the best. My freshman year, I was issued a helmet so big I could see out of the ear hole.

Our football contests were played on Friday nights until my junior year, when they were moved to Saturday afternoons. The reasons for the switch were twofold. First, it was too costly to light the field for an evening game. Beyond that, the powers that be figured that opponents were less likely to get into brawls in broad daylight.

As certain as the weekend football game was the inevitability of church on Sunday. Religion in my house was complicated. My mother's parents were German, and for them, life centered on the church. Her father was a Lutheran pastor for more than half a century, while her mother taught Sunday school and played the church organ. On top of that, they led study groups and missions. God was a full-time vocation. Life was structured and disciplined, and all of it influenced by God's word.

My father was of Scandinavian descent and was raised by his mother and stepfather. When he was five, his father met an untimely death, ironically while working in a funeral home. The owner had just received a new firearm for his gun collection and was happy to show it to my grandfather, not realizing there was a live round in it. The gun accidentally discharged, killing his thirty-year-old employee.

As a consequence of losing his father so young, my dad had to grow up before his time. Although his mother remarried, life with a stepfather was not the same. Gone was any hope for a carefree, uncomplicated childhood, and my father took on a sturdiness—some might say a sternness—that held him together for the rest of his life. My father's stepdad may not have influenced *his* life, but he would become a major influence in mine.

Our church congregation was about the same as the high school, with fewer than a hundred members. My family was one of about fifty families that attended church regularly. If I made excuses as to why I could not attend Sunday services, I was sure to be grounded for the entire day.

Seating in church was very territorial. Each Sunday, everyone assumed the same pews. I felt bad for the visitors who inevitably violated the unpublished seating chart. If the person or family whose seat was unwittingly stolen had status in the community or was a large contributor to the church, the violator would be asked, somewhat politely, to move. Other congregants would sit there, watching, horrified and shifting uncomfortably, hoping the scene would end quickly. Ideally, the visitor would just have to scoot down a bit to the other end of the pew. But if they had to actually get up and find another seat, it was almost too embarrassing to watch. The great irony to all this is that after the offerings were collected, the pastor would make a special announcement welcoming the visitors with open arms and expressing his sincere hope that they'd all return. Of course, once the sermon began, the same people who'd made certain to claim their rightful seats just as promptly and reliably fell asleep.

I never knew what it was that prompted my father to return to Malvern. Maybe he wanted his kids to be raised in a similar environment to himself, maybe it was where he could find work, maybe it was financial.

Rarely did anyone leave Malvern, and rarer still did anyone ever return. In spite of the limited opportunities, the fear of change or newfound freedom was paralyzing to most, the thought of a vast world entirely overwhelming. But Dad was a different breed who marched to his own beat.

Our first home was an old rented farmhouse adjacent to the family farm. These days, it is easy to romanticize life in the country. It is now a trope for urbanites to trade in city life for pastoral beauty and hard labor. Back then, though, YouTube and influencers weren't a thing. For me, country living at the time had its bucolic elements in terms of the sheer beauty of the surroundings, but other aspects left much to be desired.

Life in the farmhouse was harsh, even by early-1950s standards. The downstairs consisted of a kitchen heated by a pot-belly stove. I use the term "heated" loosely—it was more like a suggestion of warmth that could be accessed only by the immediate radius of the stove. It was my job to ferry lumps of coal from behind the house to keep the stove fed.

Off the kitchen was our only bathroom—a half bath kept warm by a small space heater to take the edge off the jagged Ohio winters. That little heater did its best, but it faced a formidable foe. Often, the temperatures dropped so low it was impossible to keep the room above freezing, at which point a blowtorch was enlisted to thaw the pipe. Not pipes, plural, but *pipe*. There was no hot water. Whether it was the dead of winter or midsummer, our water was always stone cold. In the summer, solar heat warmed water in a large metal tub for bathing, but in the winter, to get a good scrub meant heading up the road to my grandparents' place. That event happened every Saturday night, so we'd be fresh and clean for church the next day.

The upstairs of the house consisted of one bedroom for my parents and one for the rest of us. Sharing a bed with two brothers was, for most of the year, a source of annoyance, but in the winter, I did not mind. We would heap on as much clothing as we could manage—pajamas, socks, mittens, stocking caps—then sardine under a pile of quilts and my dad's old army blanket, which was woolen and scratchy. We lived this way for three achingly long years before Dad purchased three acres on the family farm. On that land, Dad built a three-bedroom, one-and-a-half-bath house that was fully heated and lavishly outfitted to offer both hot and cold water. The house was glorious, with one small exception.

In the late '50s, nothing about television was high tech. The majority of TVs were black-and-white, there were a handful of channels, and reception was inconsistent at best. Getting a signal required either a large antenna on the roof or a set of "rabbit ears" that sat atop the TV and had to be continually adjusted based on the channel you wanted to watch. Dad ditched the rabbit ears in favor of an outdoor antenna, only instead of mounting it on the roof or the chimney like most would have done, he opted to fix it to a dead tree that sat in an open pasture about one hundred feet from the house. The idea had some logic to it. Dad reasoned that with nothing around the antenna to obscure it, we'd get a better signal. Yet while the theory was sound, the reality left something to be desired.

When we got the antenna installed and connected, it turned out that the picture on each of the three channels was no better than with the rabbit ears. That was a disappointment, to say the least. From there, things got worse. To receive the best possible reception, the antenna had to be cajoled into alignment with the signal of the channel you wanted to watch, a process that took no fewer than three people. First, someone had to scale the barbed-wire fence into the pasture, then climb a ladder to reach the antenna. Person number two had to station themselves outside the door to the house to act as a relay, while person three would shout instructions from the television. Naturally, those duties usually fell to us kids. While such an exercise was annoying in the summer, in the winter, it was tantamount to child abuse. God finally blessed us when one day, the tree and the antenna were struck by lightning, bringing an end to both.

Growing up, I was always under the watchful eye of my father. His parenting philosophy was simple: These are the rules, and this is the punishment you will receive if they are not followed. Being that I was the oldest, very little went unnoticed. From how I held my fork at the dinner table to how I addressed my elders to how I was dressed, there was an expectation for everything. Failure to meet those expectations ranged from a good scolding to finding myself leaving the ground in one fashion or another.

When I entered high school, the list of expectations grew enormously. Dad was now my teacher, coach, and church adviser. As there was only one class for each subject, teaching full-time meant teachers oversaw many subjects. My dad taught me algebra I and II, plane and solid geometry, chemistry, and physics. He was also my junior high basketball coach and my varsity football and varsity baseball coach. There was nowhere to hide.

I did catch a break when Dad was relieved of his role as an adviser to the church youth group. He, along with two other male advisers, were responsible for driving our group to a daylong Luther League Youth rally. There were programs and speakers throughout the day for all attendees, including the advisers. Our advisers, including my dad, opted to instead take part in a less-than-holy activity. The third installment of the James Bond franchise had recently hit theaters. I guess the idea of seeing Jill Masterson naked and dipped in gold was more appealing than supervising a group of pubescent teens, because they forwent their churchly duties and opted for a viewing of *Goldfinger* instead. Upon learning of the advisers' indiscretions, the church elders promptly relieved them of their responsibilities. That was the only time my mother read my dad the riot act, and he did nothing but listen.

In the classroom and in athletics, I was disciplined and congratulated by my father the same as everyone else. The difference was when we got home. My performance, technique, attitude—everything was open to scrutiny. When he was the evaluator, there was little discussion. My response was either "Yes, sir" or "No, sir."

I was a good kid, not an angel, but the mistakes I made were commensurate with my peers and all the half-baked things you do when you're growing up. Yet I felt a constant pressure to perform. To be sure there was something to gain from this ethos. Over time, I learned to internalize this drive, and it paid off in many ways. It was not until many decades, multiple careers, and a battle with depression later that I realized there were other impacts.

The one class where I did not operate under my dad's watchful eye was music class. That position was reserved for my mother, who was the head of Malvern's music department.

My mother attended Capital University, where she majored in music. It was also where she met my dad. They were married in 1947—my mother's freshman year and my dad's senior year. Soon after graduating with a degree in civil engineering, Dad joined the US Army Corps of Engineers, serving in Korea and holding the rank of first lieutenant. By the time he was discharged in 1954, our family consisted of my parents, me (age six), my sister (age five), and my brother (age three). Another brother would be born a year later.

While at Capital, Mom earned enough college credits to receive a teacher's certification, which allowed her to teach full-time, provided that each year she take a minimum of five hours of classroom credit toward her degree. Every summer, Mom drove sixty miles three days a week for six weeks. She did that for fifteen years before she received her undergraduate degree in 1970. Throughout this time, she maintained her domestic responsibilities, as well as canning and freezing all the fruits and vegetables from our garden for the coming winter. Oh, and she welcomed a fifth addition to the family, another son, thirteen years younger than me (oops).

It was during this time that I first saw my mother's determination, commitment, and responsibility. Alongside her toughness and grit was a rock-solid pragmatism. Case in point: At thirteen, I was involved in an accident that resulted in my index finger being split open lengthwise to the bone. Without missing a beat, my mother shuttled me off to the veterinarian to have it sewn back up. Yes, the vet. The accident happened on a Wednesday afternoon, and the only doctor in the area took Wednesday afternoons off, so she contacted our livestock vet. We were not concerned about the scar, only stopping the bleeding. Mission accomplished.

All those years, Mom drove back and forth to Malone College—where she took the credits required to maintain her teaching certification—in a 1962 Ford Fairlane. It had once been a police car and still had the searchlight bolted to the driver's side door. It looked like the car used in *The Blues Brothers*.

Mom also gave piano lessons to nearly everyone in the county. Eventually she took her savings and bought a brand-new 1965 Ford Mustang, the first such car sold in the county. It was red with a red interior. She did not consult with my dad because she felt she deserved it and earned it, so she bought it.

As part of my curriculum, I was not required to take music, but when your mother is the head of the music department, you don't have a choice. I knew what I was getting into, because Mom was the choir director at church and I had been a member since I was in junior high.

My singing voice developed well enough that I entered the district solo contest at school. I qualified to audition at state. It was an audition rather than a competition because you received a grade for your individual performance, not a ranking against the competition.

I was given a list of songs from which I could select one. I chose "Oh Shenandoah."

It was late in the afternoon when I was scheduled to perform before a single judge. He had heard the song over and over that day and by then was bored to tears. Before I began my performance, he displayed his boredom by watching a pickup basketball game taking place outside the window. That turned out to be my saving grace. As I was starting the second verse, the words completely escaped me, so I repeated the first verse and then concluded with the third. Because the judge was distracted, he was unaware of what had happened and rated my performance as being superior. I took the win and never sang publicly again!

My mother was fiercely independent, held strong convictions, and was very determined. Like my dad, she showed little emotion or sympathy. Her approach to life was to deal with setbacks, adversity, and heartache, then quickly get over it.

I was driving home from my dad's funeral in 1997, when my mother announced that when she got home, she was ordering a harp. She was learning to play the harp and had been practicing and performing with a rented instrument. All the while, she would remind my dad that she wanted to buy a new harp. His reply was always the same: "Mary Anna, you can buy a goddamn harp when I am dead and buried." In the end—which was *his* end—she got her harp.

When my youngest brother took his own life at fifty years

of age, my mother's response was par for the course. "Your father is going to give him a good talking to."

For twenty-five years following my dad's death, my mother lived alone. For much of that time it was just her and her cocker spaniel, Lucky Lady. When Lucky Lady died, Mom was content with making handmade cards for special occasions, giving piano lessons, and playing the organ for nearly every wedding and funeral in the county. I taught her how to use the internet, and soon after, she complained that it was too slow.

A few months before she died, I visited my mother, and as I was leaving, she wanted to follow me so I could stop at the local gas station to show her how to use the new pumps they had just installed. She was too proud to ask any of the attendants.

In the end, my mother's only fear was losing her independence, which she fiercely protected. She died sitting in her favorite chair on a Sunday afternoon at the age of ninety-one, independence intact.

Growing up in a house where both parents have strong personalities along with high expectations and requirements can weigh heavily on a young person. Thankfully, I had an outlet.

At age eight, I started working the same fields on the dairy farm where my dad was raised. It consisted of about a hundred and twenty-five cows, and at any given time, sixty to sixty-five were being milked. In addition, on those two hundred acres, we grew hay, corn, and oats, all to feed the cows.

Now, there wasn't much an eight-year-old boy could do on a dairy farm, but free labor was never refused. Nothing on that farm was automatic, except for the milking machines and the vehicles, so most things had to be done manually. My first job was to wash the cows' udders before milking. It wasn't complicated or difficult, but it was important. Buyers would test the milk for purity, and if any bacteria entered the milk stream, it would be detected and the milk rejected. That placed the task high on the priority list.

Under most circumstances, cows tend to be fairly docile creatures, but the job wasn't without its hazards. For instance, cows have powerful tails, and they're adept at using them to swat flies. Should you fail to monitor your body's position relative to that tail, what gets swatted could be your face. On top of that, understandably, cows don't appreciate having their udders handled roughly. They're happy to communicate this by handling you roughly, with a good swift kick.

At the helm of the whole operation was Dad's stepbrother, assisted by his stepfather, Arthur, or Art, as everyone called him. When we weren't milking, I was Art's gopher. As in, "Chuck, go for my hammer!" or "Go open the gate" or "Turn the lights out," or any of a million other small tasks. In the process, I learned what needed to be done, when, and how to do it. By the time I was ten, I was turning that knowledge into action. I could not only milk the cows but also clean the stables, bale the hay, fix the fences, and drive both the tractor and the combine. For my efforts, I was paid ten cents per hour.

The days were long. When you're done milking, if you have another team helping with the work, you might be in the fields at eight thirty or nine o'clock at night. As I got older and could handle more work, including operating the vehicles, it wasn't unusual for me to spend ten hours on a tractor, often by myself, mowing the hay and then raking it into rows, plowing a field, or spreading manure to fertilize the soil.

During those times, my only company was the sound of the tractor and my own thoughts. I'd have to pay attention to make sure everything was working and I was doing the job properly, but around and around I'd go. On the positive side, my brain was on automatic pilot, freeing my mind to go anywhere I wanted it to. I trained myself to be able to think introspectively and occupy my mind without being bored, and I carried that skill through the rest of my life.

Today, I don't understand when I see people go for a walk with a headset or earbuds, or why people constantly need to be occupied or entertained by someone or something. I wonder if kids and even adults develop that skill anymore, of being able to think about things that are important rather than always having to being entertained or distracted. The ability to do so unlocks a lot.

On the farm, you also learn early on about discipline and finding a process that works. Once you find it, you make it repeatable. Those values apply to absolutely everything, though I'm not sure how skilled and capable we are at creating that kind of order these days. I sometimes question how often we stop to analyze what we're doing to see if it can be improved or systematized. Maybe we're so focused on the future that this seems like a tall order, but in farming, that's how you get from one day to the next. That's how you manage to get everything done that needs to be done and still get the cows secured in the barn before nightfall. For lots of us, our cows are still out wandering around in the pasture long after the sun sets. Yet it seems to me that if we stopped and expended the effort to look at how we're doing what we're doing, we'd make some of the hard stuff easier.

To be sure, I learned other useful skills out in those fields as well. Being able to drive a tractor around for hours on end in ninety-degree weather with the sun beating down on your head can feel monotonous, but it has to be done. There's real value in building that muscle of being able to knuckle down and do the stuff that isn't appealing but is still important. In addition to developing perseverance and the ability to be uncomfortable, it underscored for me the idea that sometimes it's not about you but about the group. Your piece of the work might not be fun or gain you any personal glory, but there's real value in contributing to a shared result.

I also developed some less tangible skills, like learning to operate a tractor while standing up, because boy does your butt get tired after a while. Also, wearing a pair of Levi's in that relentless heat, you're liable to be soaked from the waist down. The only reason my shirt wasn't drenched was because on those days, I wasn't wearing one. And unfortunately, spending all those long hours on the tractor meant I never learned how to swim. I never could learn on the privacy of the farm grounds because the only places we had water were where the cows would drink—creeks and ponds with things in them you didn't want any contact with. My feet going into that muck and mud was a feeling I just hated. There was a water park in Canton, which was about thirty miles away. My friends went from time to time, but I always demurred.

The thing was, from all those hours outdoors, I had the farmer tan to end all farmer tans. From the waist up, I was as dark as the bark on a maple tree. There wasn't a lifeguard in the country who had a better tan than I did. But from the waist down, I was as white as an aspen. There was no opportunity to even out because you didn't dare wear anything other than long pants on a farm. The upshot was that I was two-tone, and I did not need the kind of verbal abuse that would come with putting that on display for a bunch of teenagers. To this day, I'm still embarrassed remembering what I looked like.

Both my sons learned how to swim when they were two. If they were ever in danger, I needed them to be able to save themselves without relying on me.

Life on the farm felt good. For starters, farmwork got me away from home, which felt like a welcome break, but I was also earning my own money. Yet while it was empowering to start accumulating something of my own in terms of both knowledge and wealth, it was my relationship with Art that was the biggest payoff. Art was the best role model a young boy could ever have. Over the years, he became a true mentor to me—a combination role model, teacher, and confidant. He was a sage, and I was his anxious pupil, happy to soak in anything I could from this man I so admired.

Art was in his mid-eighties, his head topped with thick snowy-white hair. With 190 pounds of hard-earned muscle atop his six-foot, two-inch frame, he was an imposing figure for any age. He was a handsome man with an easy smile and looked every inch the farmer. His typical uniform was a white long-sleeve shirt with a preacher's plain collar under bib overalls, along with heavy work boots and a wide-brimmed straw hat. Hanging from his back pocket like a kid dangles out a car window on a summer drive was a red-and-gray bandanna. He never swore, and was always soft spoken.

The times I messed up, Art usually handled it with sly sarcasm. If I'd come back with the wrong tool, he'd say, "Son, the more education you get, the dumber you become." If we were building a wire fence and I hit the steeple (or staple, as non-farmers call it) wrong, it would fly off at an angle, to which Art would dryly declare, "It won't go in until you hit the head." Such commentary might seem somewhat mean these days or if you didn't know Art, but I always knew there was no real disdain behind it. In his own way, he was simply telling me to take more care.

Mucking provided more fertile ground—so to speak—for learning. We'd clean out manure from the cow stalls using pitchforks. I had a method whereby I'd take the pitchfork and lean it over my knee to pry up the packed-down manure. The thing is, when you do that, if you meet too much resistance, you're likely to break the handle. Invariably, I'd break two or three pitchforks a year. Art would just look at me and say, "Anybody who knows how to use a pitchfork would never break the handle." He wasn't wrong.

One of my favorite things was when Art would show me some of the antics he and his brothers got up to for entertainment when they were young. Necessity was the mother of invention, and they made up all kinds of games to play when there was a lull in the action. One was something they called Splits. Back then everyone had a pocketknife—it was surely a Barlow pocketknife. Two boys would stand on a wooden surface—maybe the barn floor or in a hay wagon—and face each other, spreading their legs shoulder-width apart. One would take his knife and throw it near the other's foot. If it stuck in the wood, that boy had to spread his foot to where the knife was without moving the other one. When one foot was spread out so far they couldn't reach the knife, the other was declared the winner.

They'd also stand on the prongs of a pitchfork and see who could balance longest. Plus there were the feats of strength. In one competition, they'd take a burlap sack and fill it with wheat, which is maybe one of the heaviest grains there is. The sack might weigh seventy-five to a hundred pounds and be about four feet tall. On top of that, they'd be standing in a bushel basket, which is tippy. In one move, they'd have to hoist that bag up and onto their shoulder without falling out of the basket.

They might have come up with these games as boys and teens, but you'd still see grown men playing them as well. It was like rural Ohio's version of the Scottish Highland games, picking up heavy things and seeing who could throw them the farthest. You'd see farmers who looked spindly and skinny, but I knew that this was how they entertained themselves. I certainly wouldn't have wanted to take them on for anything.

Art taught me what I needed to know. Everything from how to operate the farm machinery and the patterns required to mow hay most efficiently, to the precautions to take when baling hay on steep slopes or descending hills while pulling a loaded wagon. He taught me how to dehorn cattle, neuter hogs, and deliver newborn calves.

However, there was one thing Art tried to teach me that I wasn't so interested in learning. No matter the time of day, if you came upon Art, you'd find his left cheek swollen with a plug of Mail Pouch Tobacco. He'd drive along on the tractor, then periodically cock his head and project a bullet of spit over the left fender. On occasion, his expulsions lacked the requisite vigor, in which case there'd be more juice on the fender than on the ground. I always took a moment to examine the fender before I sat on it.

Art possessed what modern child-development experts call an authoritative style. He was patient, but held high standards. He had strong opinions, but was respectful of others. And his boundaries, like a well-built fence, were firm around the perimeter. Inside, however, there was lots of room to run.

It's a common misperception that all farmers have a strong work ethic. More accurately, that's a characteristic reserved for *successful* farmers, of which Art was certainly one. He was as consistent as the sunrise. Six days a week, he'd arrive at the barn at 5 a.m., then stay until the last milking was done. Sunday was set aside for religion and family.

Art's church attire was as distinctive as his work clothes—a three-piece suit, crisp white shirt, and tie, topped with a straw hat as milky-white as his hair. It was easy to understand why, after the death of Art's wife at age sixty-five, he was pursued by every woman in the county who was unmarried and of a certain age. He did eventually remarry, not once but twice. His second wife passed just five years after their vows. One year later, at age ninety and to the dismay of the family, he took a third wife. The day of the wedding, he leaned over and with a Cheshire grin shared with me the prediction that he'd outlive this wife as well, and marry yet again. He was half right.

Art's life did extend past that of his third bride, but he did not remarry after. Instead, he treated himself to a brand-new 1956 Packard, and she was a beaut—all white with a red interior and wide whitewall tires. The automobile was just as distinctive and classy as its driver. In retrospect, I think the old man finally realized that at that point, he'd feel both younger and happier with a new car rather than a new wife.

It was a beautiful spring day in March, and I was thirteen years old. There I was bouncing along on the school bus, headed toward home. As the first kid on the bus in the morning, I was also the last one off, and it was just me peering out over a sea of black bench seats.

We were rolling past the front yard of Art's big farm when I looked out and saw the old man lying there on the side of the hill. I shouted to the bus driver, who lurched to a stop at the base of the hill. I jumped out, telling myself that Art was just napping.

I sprinted over and dropped to my knees next to him. I leaned over, slowly turning his head toward me. As I looked down at Art's face, I saw that his eyes were open. The only reason I knew he was still breathing was the sound of the air moving, slow and shallow, in and out. Then, he took his last breath.

Beside Art sat the wooden tray that held his hand tools. He'd been on his way to repair a barn door.

From that day on, I have always tried to emulate Art's values of trust, honesty, fairness, empathy, respect, courage, and integrity. I did not fully realize it at the time, but the work ethic I was coming to develop came squarely from him. Art instilled in me a belief I carry to this day: that as long as I am standing, there is always a chance.

CHAPTER 2

From Baseball to Football

Farmers gravitate to a way of life that cannot be found anywhere else. At least, that was true of the way farming was when I was growing up. It's a lot different now that there's more automation and so much of it has been corporatized. Back then, and I'm sure still in some cases today, farming offered an opportunity to invest in yourself, for your own benefit as well as others'. You not only produced something of value with your own two hands but also improved yourself in the process. It was a pursuit that offered endless hours of satisfaction, but not without sacrifice. I'm more certain now than ever that the two go hand in hand.

What began as an escape from my life at home became a destination for experiential learning, and what I absorbed on that farm formed a foundation that supported me the rest of my life. As I grew older and as Art's legacy became more deeply ingrained in me—I metabolized his lessons all the way down to my marrow—I began to crave that sense of satisfaction that only came with doing your best. Some credit is due to my parents as well, but as life went on, I internalized that ethos and it became my own internal motivation.

In any given twenty-four-hour period, what got me up and kept me moving until the last chore was done was the gratification I knew awaited me when I climbed into bed in the evening. It was about knowing I'd done all I could. That even if I was just an eighth of an inch beyond where I'd started that day, I'd improved. It gave me a sense of peace, and of confidence.

Don't get me wrong—I was still a knucklehead. I was a teenage boy, after all. But I was on a path. I didn't know where it would take me, but it felt worth traveling. I never worried about my destination, only the investments I was making to get there.

With farming, the work was physically demanding, the hours endless, and the commitment total. Failure was a given, adversity was expected, and conceding was not an option. It was the perfect setup for sports.

At nine years of age, I was old enough to join both Little League and 4-H, a youth development organization that includes agricultural programming. Dad told me I could choose one. Any parent with a kid who does multiple activities can likely sympathize with the effort of shuttling them around, but for my dad, it also came down to gas and time.

"I'm not going to spend my day and gas money hauling you all over the county," he told me.

It's true—he was pretty frugal when it came to gasoline. With rare exceptions, we only traveled the five miles to town for school during the week, choir practice on Wednesday nights, the grocery store on Saturdays, and church on Sundays.

After some deep contemplation (as deep as a nine-year-old can manage), I opted for 4-H. Wrong choice. Dad wanted me to play baseball, so in the end, he relented and allowed me to do both. In a stroke of good fortune, one of the assistant coaches lived up the road from us, and so I tagged along to practice in the back of his pickup truck. It was a bouncy ride, but the price was right.

I made the team as starting left fielder. My hours at the farm stayed the same, except I was released from milking duties on the nights I had practice or a game. Our team was young, but we had potential. My first year, I threw right-handed, but I returned the next as a southpaw. During recess at school, we always played baseball. Well, one day, I forgot my glove, and the only one available was a leftie. Turned out I was better throwing with my left hand than my right, and I've thrown southpaw ever since.

Our team's potential finally began to be realized when I was twelve, which was my last year of eligibility. That season, I switched from outfielder to pitcher, and as a leftie, I had a natural curveball. In fact, I was throwing what I intended to be a fastball, but the way I released it created a spin that made it bend and twist in unpredictable patterns. The batters hated trying to hit it almost as much as my catcher hated trying to catch it. That year, I pitched seven no-hitters, batted .524, and hit eight home runs.

During our streak, the town was very supportive, and the local merchants sponsored new uniforms for the team. As is typical in Little League, the sponsors' names appeared on our uniforms, with each player sporting the name of a different supporter. The back of my jersey was emblazoned with the logo for Red's Bar and Grill. My mother was not pleased. She saw me in my uniform as a walking billboard promoting drinking and other nefarious behavior. Apparently God wasn't too upset, though—our record that year was 27–0.

Town residents would caravan to our away games, and the stands were packed for home games. Fans watching from their cars would honk their horns every time we made a good play. Each win was celebrated with a parade through downtown. It was a short one, though, considering it was only five blocks.

That year, we went all the way to the state tournament, and suffered a heartbreaking loss in the finals.

I'd kept up with 4-H all the while, and my last year in Little League also marked my last year in the 4-H program. The major difference was that showing cattle was an individual endeavor rather than a team sport. During my time in 4-H, I'd learned how to raise animals and prepare them to be judged at shows, the biggest being the annual county fair. There, animals were shown before judges, and those who raised them garnered awards in the form of trophies and ribbons based on their physical appearance (the animals', not mine—though we were expected to look presentable) and attributes. The handlers were also judged on showmanship.

To my final county fair, I took three Holsteins of different ages. I won first place in eight of nine possible categories, including grand champion. Age twelve was a good year!

Then, there was basketball. Junior high basketball was the first sport I played where my dad was the coach. I was the shortest player, but I had enough ball-handling and defensive skills to make first-team guard as a seventh grader. Basketball wasn't a sport anyone took particularly seriously, and not just because of our lackluster gymnasium. With so few boys in the school, we couldn't start practice until football season ended; otherwise there wouldn't be enough players. As a result, there was little time to prepare for the season.

The most memorable event of my junior high basketball career came during a game when my dad sent me to the showers after only a few minutes of play. That day also happened to be the annual day when we butchered a hog on the farm in the morning. The meat would be wrapped and placed in the smokehouse to cure for consumption the following year. It was a big event—one which was often celebrated with a glass or two of homemade wine. My uncle had these grapevines that grew on a trellis. As kids, we'd eat the grapes off the vine, but they made for a lousy snack. Not only were they full of seeds, they were also just hard to eat because the skins were so thick. You could chew on one of those things for an hour and still not make much progress. The real reward was the juice. Those grapes are what they'd use to make the wine, which on occasion was the celebratory beverage of choice on hog-butchering day.

As you'd imagine, the alcohol was typically reserved for adults, but that day, Art was so proud of me and my expertise in slicing slabs of pork into bacon strips that he gave me a glass. These days, I pretty much always limit my consumption to a nightly beer, enjoyed after a hard day's work. As a rule, I do not handle alcohol well, a lesson learned on that fateful day.

In the opening minutes of the basketball game, feeling confident, I launched two shots from about half-court. Neither came remotely close to hitting anything. My dad had seen enough and promptly exiled me to the locker room.

Basketball gave me a glimpse of what my dad was like as a coach, but nothing could truly prepare me for what lay ahead when I entered high school and became eligible for varsity football. Dad had played at Capital University and was the cocaptain his senior year. He was considered a big man on campus, and football was his sport. He knew the game, and he knew what it took to play it.

Because of our school's size, there were only enough players to field a varsity team. That meant that undersized and inexperienced players such as myself practiced every day with upperclassmen. I had to line up against boys who were shaving! It was intimidating, to say the least.

My first and most obvious obstacle was my size, or rather my lack thereof. As a freshman, I was five feet, four inches tall and weighed 130 pounds. I was the smallest boy in my class. In school pictures, I always sat in the front row with the girls. What I lacked in size, I failed to make up for in speed. When you're attempting not to get killed on the football field, diminutive and slow is not a good combination.

Compounding my problems was the fact that when I played both offense and defense, I lined up against the best player on the team. He was 210 pounds layered atop a six-foot, one-inch frame. He had one speed, and that was full throttle. He would play every play as if it were for the state championship. It took until well into basketball season before all my bruises disappeared.

I hated football. Every single day I wanted to quit, but I chose to endure the daily routings on the field rather than face my father's ire at home should I throw in the towel on his favorite sport.

That first year taught me what it takes to play football, and in the end, the player I lined up against—the one who made my life miserable—turned out to be the best role model in the game I could ever ask for. He epitomized the attitude, preparation, mentality, and dedication it took to play well, and to one's fullest ability. I used his benchmarks as my standard at every level of competition in which I went on to participate.

Yet to become a better player, I needed to grow in more than just my attitude, and grow I did. My sophomore year, I gained two inches and thirty-five pounds. I became a starting linebacker and offensive guard, and was selected to the all-conference team. I saw the benefits of the work I was putting in, which made me want to put in more. I realized there were definite advantages of being bigger, faster, and stronger than the competition, so I made a conscious effort to improve in each of those categories. Fortunately, my life on the farm and my attitude of continual improvement prepared me perfectly for this pursuit.

The farm provided plenty of opportunities to get bigger and stronger. There was always plenty of work to do, along with an unlimited supply of fresh milk, homegrown vegetables and fruits, and prime meats. Over my high school career, I shoveled grain, dug postholes, and handled over twelve thousand bales of hay a year, all while wearing ankle weights. For cardio conditioning, whenever I had to get from one place to another, I'd sprint, no matter the distance.

We ended my junior season undefeated. We were conference champs and ranked tenth in our state by school size. I was again selected to the all-conference team and made honorable mention for All-State.

As devoted as I became to football, baseball was still my first love, and I continued my career in high school. I was still primarily a pitcher and found that my added size and strength improved my throwing speed. Back at the beginning of my junior year, a handful of scouts from pro teams began to keep an eye on me. While I had an affinity for both sports, the decision I'd eventually face was about to be made for me.

There was a big wild grapevine that snaked up behind our house. I grew up swinging on that tall vine, suspending myself about twenty feet or so above the ground. It was a lot of fun, until the day the vine snapped. I dropped to the ground like a sack of grain, landing solidly on my left elbow. After that, I was never able to pitch more than a few innings before I was too sore to continue. I was devastated. At the same time, though that injury took baseball from me, it offered something in return—the gift of clarity. I had little choice but to take all my hopes and dreams and focus them on football.

My entire life didn't revolve around sports and the farm. Somehow, I also made time to be a typical teenage boy. That's a benefit of not having social media or smartphones—there's more time. Still, I wouldn't have minded having my own phone, or even just a little privacy. There was no such thing in my house, especially when it came to the telephone. The only phone was in the kitchen, which was centrally located downstairs. Our phone connection was what was called a party line, the same line being shared by five other families, any one of whom could pick up the phone and listen in on whatever conversation was happening at the time. A party, it was not.

To make a call, you asked an operator to connect you to the person you wanted to reach. Yes, the person, not the number. No one had a phone number, only a personal ring. Ours was two longs and a short. When you heard the ring and picked up the phone, the operator would make the connection. If you ever saw the old skit on *Laugh-In* with Lily Tomlin as the operator ("One ringy dingy . . ."), it was pretty much like that. Our household phone system didn't come into the twenty-first century until after I left for college. Needless to say, I was behind the curve when it came to mastering the art of telephonic communication.

The party line wasn't the only impediment to my dating life. At sixteen, I finally got my driver's license, and that opened up social opportunities. Yet when there are only eleven girls in your class, all of whom you've known since first grade, the prospect of dating isn't quite as compelling. There's little of the intrigue and curiosity that typically sparks early forays into courting.

My parents further limited the dating pool with an edict that I date only Protestant girls, preferably Lutheran. That decreased my prospects to a grand total of three.

There were neighboring towns, of course, but meeting the girls there wasn't easy. That was, unless they were in 4-H, went to cattle auctions, or hung out at the feed mill. And, for reasons that may be apparent, those probably weren't the girls who would set my heart to racing.

Dances were out of the question because from an early age, it was evident that I had no rhythm. This was not an overstatement, as anyone in the Steubenville, Ohio, television viewing area could have affirmed.

Steubenville was about thirty-five miles from Malvern, and one of the local TV stations there hosted a weekly dance show. It was Saturdays at noon, and it was called *NineTeenTime*. Local high schools were invited to participate, which involved showing up and dancing on the set to good old rock-and-roll music. Now, I loved rock and roll—that wasn't the issue. On the farm, the first thing the first person to enter the barn in the morning would do was switch on the radio. At the end of the day, the last one out would turn it off. But sadly, an affinity for music doesn't necessarily translate to an ability to dance to said music.

Well, one week, my high school was invited to be on the show. The teachers selected fifteen girls from the junior and senior classes, and they in turn each selected a male partner. One of the girls who'd been chosen was our class president, and she was six feet tall. Since I was the only boy taller than she was, I was the natural choice. Unfortunately for both of us, there was nothing I could do or say to get out of it. And with us both being so, let's say, *noticeable*, there was nowhere on the dance floor for us to hide. We stood out like giraffes among sheep.

To make matters worse, which I wasn't sure was even possible, at the end of the show, we were instructed to form a line. The idea was that the host would go down the row and ask each of us our name, then present us with a gift certificate from the program's sponsor, a local fast-food restaurant. The host got one look at me and, after I introduced myself, declared, "By the size of you, I'm giving you two gift certificates!" I was mortified. In all, it was the most humiliating half hour of my life, and the whole community, not to mention scores of strangers, had a front-row seat.

In spite of these hurdles, I managed to make my way to senior year, and put on a few more inches and pounds in the process. By graduation, I'd gone from the runt of the litter to six foot three and 230 pounds. But before I got there, the next of several major and unexpected life changes was about to greet me.

Going into senior year, life had an order and a flow. There was an evenness to it. My daily schedule rarely changed. I saw the same people in the same places doing the same things. Much like riding a merry-go-round, the scenery never changed, and I was having a pretty good time. That was, until my father was fired as assistant coach.

My dad's dismissal was not a complete surprise. Our head coach didn't relate well to the team, and my father did. The head coach resented the respect the team had for my dad and their relationships with him. Things with the head coach got so bad that we took a vote and agreed to boycott the next season if he was not replaced. As a cocaptain, I was chosen to present our position at the next meeting of the school board. Our proposal, such as it was, was rejected, and my father was fired.

This wasn't just a bump in the road or a form of tough luck I'd just have to deal with—it meant I'd have to change schools. Not playing football was not an option. This created a major upheaval in my life. Not only would I have to leave the town I grew up in and the team I'd grown up with, but it wasn't easy to pull off. The only way I could transfer schools without losing my last year of eligibility to play sports was for my family to establish residency in that district. The other high school in our county—Carrollton High School—was the only option. It was only twelve miles from our home, but it was also a world away. Carrollton's senior class was literally ten times the size of my class at Malvern—two hundred and forty students compared to twenty-four. But their science classes were equipped with microscopes and their gym had glass backboards!

Our solution was to rent a three-bedroom house a few blocks from the school. It was so small you could plug a vacuum into one outlet and clean the whole house without switching plugs. The last thing my parents wanted to do with this whole arrangement was to spend a lot of money on a rental. All we needed was something that had some kind of kitchen and where the roof didn't leak. Every Sunday night, we packed our things for the week and traveled to our temporary home, then returned after Friday night's football game.

For their parts, my siblings didn't complain. It could have been because they understood and were supportive, but more likely it was just the general attitude in our house that if something was inevitable, it didn't make sense to complain about it. You just went along and made whatever adjustments you needed to make. There was a silver lining, though, in that gone was the one-hour bus ride. Since we were now closer to school, we got to enjoy a bit more sleep each morning.

My dad took a job procuring property for a land-development company in the Midwest. That meant that he was now traveling during most weeks, but he'd always manage to make it home for the games. Then he'd stay on with us through the weekend and head out again on Monday.

Back in Malvern, as luck would have it, the head coach ended up resigning. It didn't change my decision, but it did enable my old teammates to play their senior season, for which I was grateful.

This all sounds a lot smoother than it felt. In many ways, I was rocked to the core. The ground beneath my feet had shifted, and I struggled to find balance. I had to find a way to right the ship so I could make the most of my new circumstances, so I did what I've done in so many challenging and disorienting situations since—I got focused. I zeroed in on what was under my control, isolating the immediate and short-term actions I could take to restore my sense of confidence and calm, and to get me thinking logically instead of emotionally. You don't recover from sudden change overnight. It takes time, along with patience and a positive attitude. It was hard to adjust, but adjust I did.

I reported to my first practice with my new team another ten pounds heavier. All told, in four years, I'd grown eleven inches and gained one hundred pounds. Parents of toddlers have a heck of a time keeping their kids in clothes. One morning, that toddler can put on a pair of shoes that fit the night before and find their toes nearly bursting out. I was reliving a bit of that, going through new clothes every three months. My transformation was particularly evident one Easter Sunday.

On Easter, your regular Sunday best wasn't good enough. You had to have something new. That year, my Easter finery included a fresh Palm Beach sport coat in lime green. Needless to say, I was a sight. I was so proud when I pulled on that blazer, but it didn't even make it through the service. After the sermon, as everyone shifted in their seats, I reached out to stretch my arms. If you ever saw the opening to *The Incredible Hulk*, you can imagine what happened next. That lime-green blazer of mine split right down the back, top to bottom. That was the last time the sport coat saw the light of day, but what a glorious thirty minutes it had been.

At Carrollton, I was the biggest player on the team, and there was only one pair of uniform pants that fit me. On the first day of practice, while the rest of the team showed up in their white pants, I was the lone player in purple. So much for not wanting to draw attention.

Because I was new to the team, I had to earn a starting position. I began the first practice as the second-team offensive tackle and second-team linebacker. After our first scrimmage,

I was promoted to the starting slot for both positions. It was then, and only then, that I was accepted as an official member of the team.

Expectations for that season were that the team would do about as well as they'd done in the past—somewhere in the neighborhood of five hundred. We surprised everyone by winning our first eight games, and surprised them even more by holding our opponents scoreless during the first seven. We ended with a record of 8–1–1.

As heartbreaking and flat-out traumatic as it had been to change schools and to adjust to a different lifestyle and surroundings, there would be, as I'd learn, profound benefits to this shift. It's not overstating matters to say it changed the entire course of my life.

It was always expected that I'd attend college, most likely the same university as my parents. It wasn't simply a matter of family pride—Lutherans received a $300 annual scholarship, which counted for a lot in those days. But playing at Carrollton against a higher level of competition, and for a winning team, raised my profile. Scouts were starting to look at me as I began to attract attention from Division I schools. Eventually, I was invited to visit schools in the Big Ten, the Ivy League, and the Academies. In the end, I accepted invitations from Indiana and Michigan State.

Indiana hosted a recruiting weekend during which all twenty-seven players they were actively recruiting visited at the same time. When we arrived, we assembled in a room where we were paired with an escort for the weekend. I watched as every other recruit was paired with a varsity player to act as their host and guide for the weekend. When it was only me left, all the varsity players had already been matched. My escort was to be the head cheerleader. I was speechless. Later, I learned that they'd wanted to make a particularly good impression on me, and as a result, I spent the next two days in the company of the most beautiful creature I'd ever seen.

Upon my return home, I announced I was going to Indiana.

After I told my parents about my weekend, and my host, my parents realized that my infatuation was less about the school and more about the student body. One student body in particular. The fact that she was all I talked about was most likely what gave me away.

Soon after my return, I received a letter from the cheerleader expressing how much she had enjoyed our time together. I sure hope that after graduation she went into sales.

Patiently, Dad pointed out to me that by the time I got to Indiana, my crush would likely be long gone. Eventually, I came to my senses and agreed to consider other options.

Incidentally, I may not have seen that young woman again at Indiana, but she did reenter my life about fifty years later, albeit in a roundabout way. My wife and I were having dinner with a couple in Asheville, North Carolina, at their house. The husband had gone to Indiana, so I told him the story of my memorable recruiting weekend. He looked at me for a moment, then stood up from the table and disappeared. A short time later, he returned, carrying an Indiana yearbook with "1967" emblazoned on the cover. As he held out the yearbook, my gaze landed on a picture of that same cheerleader. I nearly fell out of my chair. I hadn't imagined her, after all!

My Michigan State recruiting weekend was far less memorable, and far less enjoyable. My host there was a varsity lineman who was every bit the stereotype of a dumb jock. I wanted more out of college than to be on a winning team. Back then, getting recruited was a big deal not because we were thinking about our egos or the NFL, but because it was a ticket to a first-rate education, and a scholarship. Even though I didn't know what my long-term goals were, I knew they'd require a solid education, and I was anxious to acquire one. So after that experience, Michigan State was easy to eliminate.

Indiana was once again in the lead, but then another candidate came forward. Three weeks before the college deadline to sign high school seniors to scholarships, I heard from Ohio State. It was the first time they'd reached out. As it turned out, our county judge had contacted head coach Woody Hayes. The judge had lived in Woody's dormitory when they were both students at Denison University. I first came onto this judge's radar under some less-than-positive circumstances.

When my mother got her brand-new Mustang, for a time, she refused to let me drive it, though I was salivating to do so. Then, one day, as we were getting ready to leave to pick up my dad from the airport in Canton, she announced she was going to let me drive. I'd been driving for years on the farm, but I'd just gotten my official license, and so it was a celebration of sorts.

We weren't even out of the city limits before I saw a set of flashing lights. This was a time when kids would drag race their muscle cars on the weekends. A highway patrolman saw us go by with me at the wheel. Seeing an opportunity to rid the streets of one of these hell-raising kids, he slipped out right behind us. He pulled us over and decided to write me a ticket for two minor infractions he claimed I'd committed: not coming to a complete stop at a stop sign and veering slightly over the center line on a curve.

Back then, in our county, if you were under eighteen and received a traffic violation, they automatically gave you a fine and confiscated your license for two months. My mother took me to my court hearing, and as the judge reviewed the facts of my case, I already had my license out of my wallet, ready to hand it over. Homecoming and all the events that came with it were disappearing before my eyes.

I knew who the judge was because his twin daughters were

in school with me. I didn't realize that Judge Richards knew who I was, or that he was a football fan. In just a few days, the team would face Minerva—the biggest rivals on our schedule.

Judge Richards looked down from his bench. "Were you guilty of these violations?" he asked.

"Well, I didn't see it the same way the officer did," I said, trying to be diplomatic and respectful of authority even though I knew the charges were petty. "The reason I maybe didn't come to a complete stop was that I could see a few miles down in either direction, and it was obvious the road was clear."

He thought about it for a minute and then asked me another question: "Are we gonna beat Minerva this week?"

My heart jumped. "I *guarantee* we're gonna beat Minerva!" I declared.

"All right," he said, "that'll be a fifty-dollar fine. Pay it on the way out."

Grinning from ear to ear, I slipped my license back into my wallet. Thank you, Judge Richards!

We did beat Minerva, 20–0. I intercepted a pass that helped to ensure our shutout.

At some point afterward, Judge Richards contacted his old classmate, then the head coach at Ohio State. "We've got this big old farm boy who's been kicking the shit out of everybody, but we really don't know how good he is because he's so much bigger and faster than everybody else," he told Coach Hayes. "I think someone should take a look at him."

The assistant coach responsible for recruiting my region watched some film, then he came and saw me play basketball. He was impressed not so much with my basketball skills but with the combination of my size and how I moved on the court. OSU was officially interested.

Coach Hayes came to our house to meet me and speak with my parents. During his two-hour visit, he addressed most of his conversation to my mom and dad, which I thought was odd. Wasn't I the one he wanted to woo? Later, I learned his philosophy. The way he saw it, the parents spent more time with the players than anyone else did. If he could convince the parents that Ohio State was the best pick, they were likely to try to convince their son of the same belief. It worked, because a week later, I accepted Ohio State's twenty-first and last scholarship for the Class of 1966.

Years later, my mom told me I'd actually dreamed of attending Ohio State. I'd forgotten all about it until she hauled out my old senior yearbook and showed me the back page. We had to list our goals and ambitions, and off the top of my head, I'd decided to say the most outlandish things I could think of. I was going to play for Ohio State, become an All-American, then play for the Cleveland Browns. Well, that was one checkmark on the board, with two more to go.

My signing was big news in my new town, and back in Malvern. When I committed to Ohio State, I became the first person in the county to accept a full athletic scholarship to a Division I school. I'd love to say the folks back home threw me a ticker-tape parade, but the reaction from the community was less than spirited. Some people were genuinely happy for me, to be sure. But among the many who were encouraging when they thought I'd attend Capital or some other similar-size college, many were less enthusiastic to see that my star had risen. The way they saw it, playing for OSU would raise my status above theirs, and they weren't too happy about that. They didn't want to see me as better than them. Of course, that's not at all how I saw myself, but that's just how some people think.

One of the ways they expressed their disapproval was by openly voicing their skepticism about how likely I was to succeed in such a competitive program. They figured I had overstepped my capabilities and my potential. The town gossip was that I would end up leaning on the parking meters in front of Coley's—the local watering hole—with those who'd never left.

As in my father's generation, most of the people I grew up with in Malvern never left. They knew in high school they were going to stay, and they looked forward to it. A few joined the military, and a small handful, like me, went to college, but that was it. Everyone else stayed there and they're still there. Their kids are there, too. It's like the Twilight Zone.

All through college, every time I came back to town to visit, I'd pass Coley's and see those men leaning on those parking meters. I was scared as hell of proving all the naysayers right. It was the greatest motivation to succeed that a guy could ask for.

CHAPTER 3

Life's Lessons . . .
in Six Minutes

Ohio State's reputation for producing winning teams attracted some of the best talent in the country. If I didn't know that before, it was immediately evident when I read the backgrounds of my fellow players.

Some of my new teammates had set state performance records, and many were awarded All-State honors, but not only in football. Several had also accrued accolades in wrestling, track and field, baseball, and basketball. My roommate, Ted Provost, was All-State in football, basketball, and track. A few were All-Americans. Sure, I'd garnered some awards of my own, but they paled in comparison. I sincerely doubt anyone lost a moment of sleep at the prospect of lining up against a two-time All-Tuscarawas County honoree. I didn't know what was waiting for me when I would show up for practice in the fall, but now I knew *who* was waiting for me. That gave me all the incentive I needed to do my best to prepare for the upcoming season. Well, nearly my best.

Ohio State's conditioning coach sent me a detailed training program, which I followed religiously. I'd finish my farmwork for the day, then lift weights and run sprints or agility drills. Some nights, my workouts ran so late they ended under the spotlights in the yard.

In all this, there were two major flaws in my routine. The first was the bugs. At night, swarms of gnats, mosquitos, and moths migrated to the lights. As I grew tired, huffing and puffing harder to force air in and out of my lungs, inevitably I inhaled insects as well. My mouth became like a Hoover for bugs.

The second shortcoming in my training was my preparation for the six-minute mile. The conditioning coach had alerted me that, upon arrival, all players would be expected to complete this run, and failure to do so was not an option. This would be no big deal for, say, a cornerback, but athletes my size are built for short bursts of power, not running distances. Anything beyond a hundred yards, and I had to pace myself. Beyond a quarter mile, I needed to stop and rest. Additionally, the road winding past my house was the only hard surface available to me where I could practice distance running with any frequency, and it was hilly, with multiple steep sections. Not ideal for distance training. These factors formed my excuse for undertraining.

One week before I was due to report for fall practice, I figured I'd better see where I stood. The only track in the county was a half-mile racetrack at the county fairgrounds, so that's where I headed, coaxing my sister to come along as my timer. The track was typically used for horse races and tractor-pulling contests. I'd have opted to pull a tractor in a heartbeat if it would've gotten me out of what I was really there for. As it was, when we arrived, we were greeted by a dozen or so harness horses that were also in training. The county fair was coming up, and the riders were getting the equines ready. The result was that I spent the first half mile dodging both horses and horse shit. As I chugged past my sister, she shouted out a time of three minutes and forty seconds. I knew there was no way I was going to complete the second half faster than the first, so I quit. My sister says I swore all the way home.

As Ohio State inched closer, my stress level crept higher. The pressure, fear, and anxiety I felt became so intense it was nearly palpable. Here I was, a few days from attempting something I'd never before accomplished, and in front of my new coaches. It would form their first impression of me, and it wouldn't be a good one.

Then, the day of my departure arrived. I'd arranged to ride to Columbus with Ted, who lived about thirty miles from me. As we were about to leave, my dad pulled me aside. He looked me square in the eyes. His only advice was this: "You know the difference between right and wrong," he said. "I did my job. Deciding whether you do right or do wrong is yours." And with that, he turned and went back into the house. At that moment, I knew that for the rest of my life, I was on my own.

We arrived safely to campus, and I found my way to the football dormitory, where I unpacked my things. You'd think the details of my first day of training camp would be chiseled in stone in my memory, but it was all a blur. The only thing I could think about was what awaited me the next morning.

After a sleepless night, I assembled with the team at the track inside the Ohio State stadium. My eyes landed on Coach Hayes, standing there in his standard uniform: a black baseball hat with a scarlet block-font O outlined in white, pulled down so the brim practically rested on his eyebrows. As I'd learn, when Woody really got pissed, he'd grab the bill of that cap and yank it down even lower. That's when you knew all hell was about to break loose. Along with the hat and his wire-rimmed glasses, he sported a gray T-shirt with "Ohio State Athletic Department" emblazoned across the chest in big red letters, then long coaching pants and black low-cut football cleats. Oh, and of course, a whistle.

For games, he wore his block cap, a short-sleeve white shirt with the top button undone, a scarlet-and-gray tie with the knot pulled down about three inches, black dress pants, and high-top football shoes. Regardless of whether it was ninety-five degrees out or a wind chill of negative twenty-five and snow, his attire never varied until my senior year. One bitter cold and windy afternoon in the Horseshoe, just before half-time, there was a murmur in the stands as if something un-believable had just taken place. As I looked around trying to understand what I'd missed, I spotted Woody. He was stand-ing there on the sidelines wearing a big, bulky winter parka. Later, as we were about to leave the locker room after halftime, he exclaimed, "I never knew a coach who was worth a damn when he was freezing his ass off." That was that.

The only other time Woody's attire changed was when he had to put on a coat and tie for a special event. I think he'd have worn his field outfit if he could have gotten away with it.

On that first day at training camp, as I took in the picture of my new head coach, I felt my heart pounding in my ears. The man was a legend. He'd taken that role at OSU in 1951, and by the time I arrived, he'd already won two national cham-pionships. When he went on to retire in 1978, he'd added a third. On top of that, he won thirteen Big Ten championships, had teams in eight Rose Bowl games, and developed fifty-eight All-American players. It was one thing sitting with Woody in my living room as he chatted with my parents. It was quite another seeing him out on the track, inside the stadium where he'd led so many teams to victory. But there was no time for stargazing—we had business to attend to.

Wasting no time, Coach Hayes promptly informed us that the penalty for failing to run the required distance in the required time would result in an opportunity to try again. Any player who did not meet the standard would have to report to the track the next day at 5:30 a.m., and they would continue this routine until they were successful. I could tell by his tone, which was somehow both flat and razor sharp at the same time, he was dead serious. I felt the panic well up inside me. I had such a high level of respect for Woody that it bordered on terror. Visions of those parking meters in front of Coley's materialized in my mind.

The coaches divided the team into groups by position. Mine comprised fifteen offensive and defensive linemen. As the lumbering horde lined up at the starting line, I devised my race strategy. It boiled down to one objective: Don't stop. I tried to harness my emotions and use them as a catalyst to succeed, or at least not to fail too miserably. Somehow, I was going to run these four laps in six minutes. I would be that mother who summoned superhuman strength to lift a car off her immobilized toddler. To succeed would likely require that magnitude of miracle.

The sharp tweet of a whistle sounded and off we went. We looked like a herd of stampeding buffalo, only much slower. I ran the first lap on a combination of adrenaline and fear. As we rounded into the start of the second lap, I was positioned in the middle of the pack, but then, one by one, other players began to pass me. I couldn't tell if it was because they were speeding up or I was slowing down. Likely, it was both.

By the third lap, I had fallen into the back third of the group. It was then that the pain really started to register. My hamstrings were so tight that my strides became shorter and shorter. Perhaps mercifully, my tailbone had gone completely numb. Every time I went to push off the ground, it felt like my feet were in quicksand. My lungs felt like someone had turned on a flamethrower inside them. My neck arched, head facing up toward the sky as I gulped for air. It looked like I was searching the heavens for help. I probably should've been.

Starting that final lap, it felt like it might be my last lap ever. Rigor mortis was setting in. At that point, I was doing all I could to just keep going. I might not make six minutes, but I wasn't going to quit. Not in front of my new coaches and teammates. Failing is human, but quitting is unforgivable. Then, about two hundred yards from the finish line, I heard a voice cry out. "You can do it. You can do it!" the voice screamed in my ear. It was the coach who'd recruited me. He ran down the track to meet me, and did all he could to help me summon every bit of energy I could muster.

The finish line was a blur in the distance, but that blur was getting closer. As we approached it, I heard the timer yelling: "Five fifty-three! Five fifty-four!" Realizing humiliation was not inevitable—that because, as Art had taught me, I was standing, there was still a chance—I gathered every ounce of energy I could and lurched toward the line, literally diving for the finish. My body pitched across at a time of five fifty-eight. Unable to force my muscles to fire, I lay there until one of the trainers rolled me onto the infield. It was over an hour before I could get up. To this day, the ghost of that physical pain still lingers in my body and my mind, but at least I avoided the emotional pain.

Years later, I asked Woody what the point was for requiring the six-minute mile—a routine we repeated at the start of every season. "Coach," I said, "we both know there's nothing about the six-minute mile that's applicable to football. What we do has nothing to do with endurance."

What he told me was one of those insights I filed away for the future. He said, "The only reason we ran the six-minute mile was because, first of all, it didn't come naturally to most of the guys on the team. If you demonstrated to me that you were willing to put in the time and the sacrifice to meet that standard, then I knew you were dedicated mentally and emotionally to do what it would take for us to win a championship. That's why I did it—so you could show me what I was looking for." Then he smiled and added, "I also knew that the anticipation would wear on you, so it would keep your mind on training and on football."

Over the next four years I would learn a lot at Ohio State—plenty in the form of traditional schooling, but much of the wisdom I took with me into the world came not from the classroom but the gridiron. During my Ohio State experience, though I certainly improved as a player, the real learning was broader than that. It was about life. And Coach Hayes was the source of much of that knowledge. Fortunately, I was smart enough to listen. The farm had prepared me for that. I became a sponge at Ohio State, and much of what I absorbed there formed the foundation for many of my decisions moving forward.

On the farm, I was taught to respect elders and listen to what they had to say. We've lost a lot of that today, with younger folks often thinking we older folks are out of touch and couldn't possibly understand the struggles of today. I'm not saying I'm the wisest of the lot, but as a culture, we lose out when we overlook the hard-earned lessons of those who've come before us. It's okay to question what you're told—there's a kind of wisdom in that—but not to listen at all means you're probably missing a lot. Luckily for me, I was raised with that ethos of trying to absorb everything I could. It helped that my first real mentor was Art, who pretty much always offered words worth hearing, even if just to generate a laugh. With Woody and his team, the knowledge ran similarly deep, and fortunately for me, I knew to pay attention.

Recently, I saw a video of Woody online. He was in a locker

room, delivering a speech. It didn't matter what year that video was from—I'd heard the same speech myself multiple times. Almost without exception, every day Woody would offer these pearls of wisdom. By my senior year, I could repeat some of the speeches essentially verbatim. A favorite was his version of my dad's old adage of "Always do your best." In Woody's lingo, it went like this: "Anyone who tells you how good you are, kick 'em in the shins—they're only making you soft!" Another was, "Sit in front of the classroom so the teacher knows you're there to learn."

Other speeches were focused on our behavior off the field. The weekend before the official start of the season, we were allowed to go home, a bit like soldiers getting leave before being shipped off to war. Of course, the stakes weren't as high for us, but playing for Woody, you often felt like they were. That weekend would be our last opportunity to go home before January, and Woody knew his boys would want to make the most of it, so to speak. All four years I played for Woody, he always gave the same talk before our departure.

"Gentlemen," he'd say, "a stiff dick has no conscience. I want no babies." He was never one to talk for twenty minutes when two simple sentences would do. We all got it, and we acted accordingly. Yes, sir!

I didn't have an issue with authority. Most of us on the team felt similarly because we were raised similarly. Many of my teammates had come from farms as well. There, you had to accept that you weren't in control. You had to adjust to the elements because someone else was always setting the thermostat. You did your best, and you took responsibility for the results.

By and large, college football programs of today are unrecognizable from what I experienced. One of my good friends from Ohio State went on to spend forty-seven years as an assistant coach in Division I schools. We still talk frequently, often discussing the current state of college ball. It's a completely different animal. For one, if you don't like your coach or you're simply not good enough to compete, you have the option to just transfer. Instead of being accountable for your own performance, you can go somewhere else and blame someone else. Back in my day, transferring was rare. You had your lot, and you worked with it. If you wanted the situation to improve, generally that meant you had to improve. But now, so many players are quick to look outside themselves, and they're encouraged to do so by agents and others, who tell them their only problem is that they're underappreciated.

The same trend seems to hold in the world off the field. If you don't like your boss or you're underperforming, in many cases, you can just get a new job. Just buff up your résumé, and move on. But you can't outrun a lack of personal responsibility. You'll just be going around in circles, never truly progressing. Sure, we're not always in the best situations, and sometimes moving on really is the best thing, but I think we often go there too quickly without looking in the mirror. Instead, we can start by asking ourselves what our role is. We can reflect on how things might change if we shift our attitude or our approach. If we work harder or smarter. If we start listening to people who have more experience than we do.

At Ohio State, I never questioned authority, at least not outwardly. Even if I didn't flat-out agree with an instruction or didn't understand why we were doing something, I trusted our coaching staff, so I assumed there was a solid reason behind it. Because with Woody, there was a reason for absolutely everything. He didn't have you go out and do things just for the sake of doing them. There was always a strategy or a rationale at play. Take the fumble drill, for instance.

At one point during the season, we'd experienced several days of rain in a row—so much that there was standing water on the field. And I'm not talking about just a few puddles.

If you went face-down in one of them, you'd almost drown. Well, Woody saw that foul scene as an opportunity—as a great time for different units to experience what it would be like to play in those conditions. He would say, "If you're going to play in the North Atlantic, you've got to practice in the North Atlantic." Each unit focused on tasks pertinent to their positions. Whatever would be hardest for you in that weather was what they simulated. Receivers and QBs did passing drills, and kickers and punters practiced handling the ball. Because fumbles likely meant the offensive line would dive on the ground recovering footballs.

After the drills, we went into the locker room. We couldn't practice anymore because the water on the field made it impossible to do anything else. That was another lesson: Don't ever tell Woody that something can't be done. The next thing we knew, as we were standing there in the locker room, we heard a God-awful roar. When we looked outside, we saw three helicopters hovering in the sky. Woody had called the governor, who in turn had called out the National Guard. The birds maneuvered in such a way that their propellers blew the water right off the field, drying it enough so we could resume practice. It was the first time I'd ever seen a helicopter. At least, that close.

There we were, already muddy and soaked to the bone from the fumble drill, and it was time to go out and do it some more. But you had to respect Woody's determination, and be impressed by his connections! The point was that our coaches wanted us to get as uncomfortable as possible. During the fumble drill, for instance, they wanted us to get used to being on the ground so we wouldn't avoid it during a game.

That was probably one of the biggest lessons I took from my time at OSU—that there's real value in being willing to be uncomfortable. This was also reinforced by the mile run, conditioning, and sprints to exhaustion. Not everyone is willing to go there. If you are, it automatically distinguishes you. You've developed something others haven't, and probably never will. It's like the guys who play football in Green Bay. When they're asked how they deal with intense cold, they say, "Eh, you get used to it." They're lying—they're always cold. The difference is that they've learned not to let it bother them mentally. They just go out there and do what needs to be done, and that attitude and skill set was learned early on. Don't tell me about the storm, just bring in the ship.

The only time Woody would ever leave the practice field was if he knew that lightning was in the area. He'd blow his whistle, and everyone would clear the field immediately. The first time I experienced this was when I was a freshman. The sky was darkening, and suddenly there was lightning in the distance. Woody sounded the whistle. "Everybody in!" he shouted. In the locker room, I took off my jersey and my pads and started getting undressed. One of the cocaptains looked at me quizzically.

"Hutch, what're you doing?" he asked.

"He called practice," I said, not sure why I had to explain what seemed evident.

"No," the cocaptain said, his voice calm and patient, as if he was attempting to explain something to a five-year-old, "he postponed practice." After about two hours cooling our heels in that locker room, the sky cleared. Then, we went back out on the field and started practice again, from the top. I was uncomfortable, all right, but I worked it out.

When something's difficult or just plain unappealing, our initial impulse is typically to look for ways to make it easier or abandon it completely. Sometimes that makes sense. Why stand in a grocery line behind three other people when there's another lane open? But in other circumstances, it's worth hanging in. You gain something meaningful from wrestling it out. Self-discovery is life's greatest teacher.

In business, when I was leading my own team, members would often come to me and ask for guidance. Maybe they were working on a presentation and didn't know where to start. Instead of giving them my input, I'd send them back to their desk. "Wrestle with it a bit," I'd say, "then come back and see me." No one's going to learn from someone just telling them what to do. That's some of the beauty of sports—at the end of the day, it's you on the field or the court or the track. If you're going to perform well, you've got to have internalized the knowledge and the skills to do so. Your coach can't do it for you.

I don't know what progress or improvement you can make in life without experiencing discomfort. The road ahead is always new territory. To get where you're going will require you to go places you've never been before, to do things you've never done. People have asked me if it's about being willing to take risks, but I don't think that's it, and the unknown might not actually end up containing any real risks. It's more about being able to accept and move into the unknown. It's a lot like all those people I know who never left Malvern. Some of them were probably happy there, in their own way, but I'm willing to bet that more of them just didn't want to leave the known.

I understand that, because hard work is hard work. Nothing's going to make it easy. There were plenty of times, both on the farm and on the field, that I sure as heck didn't want to do something. And my immediate internal reaction was just like anyone else's. Woody or one of the coaches would tell me to do something, or maybe it was Art back on the farm. Some part of my psyche would react: "I'm not doing that!" But then another part of me would step forward, and that part looked a lot like Spanky from *The Little Rascals*. In the *Our Gang* series, when faced with an unappealing task, at some point Spanky would sigh and say, "If ya gotta, ya gotta." Then he'd put his head down and do it. I was similar.

I can honestly say that in my life, it was exceptionally rare that I didn't do something that needed to be done. In spite of my initial reluctance, deep down I knew that not doing it was not really a choice. Not if I wanted to be my best. Did I want to do that fumble drill, and any number of other backbreaking, muscle-scorching drills they came up with? No, but I knew they'd make me better, and that was something I wanted. Did I want to be out on the tractor late at night being eaten alive by mosquitos? Of course not, but someone had to be. The work had to get done, or a whole cascade of other things couldn't happen. Perhaps even worse, if you quit or shirked your responsibility often enough, that action could turn into a habit.

The thing is, I don't think you can obtain anything worth getting if you're unwilling to do the work. Put yourself out there, and go against what those initial instincts tell you—those fears or that voice that says, "I'm not doing that!" What helps is trying it a few times and then reaping the rewards. It's feeling the payoff. Once you do that, you'll realize there's something on the other side of your own discomfort, and it's worth getting. You get a sense of what the reward will be or how you'll feel if you do it.

The rewards might feel relatively small sometimes, but they're rewards nonetheless. Today, after a day of hard work laying pavers or digging holes outside, I'll sit back and enjoy a beer, and I can tell you that beer wouldn't taste nearly as good if someone else did the work. That's why it's called happy hour.

One of the things Woody was so good at was training that reward circuitry—combining the discomfort we'd endure with something positive to make that experience expand. To get you past where you were. Suffering is senseless if, when it's over, you don't end up somewhere else—if you don't improve in some way, whether it's physically or mentally.

Everyone thinks they're doing the best they can until they're challenged. Until someone puts them in an environment that will take them to the next level, and that's what Woody did. He didn't just ride us into the ground, he also recognized when we did well.

One way he'd do that was with Buckeye leaves.

We played our games on Saturdays. Then every Sunday, we'd gather to watch the film. On Monday, we'd come in from practice, take off our pads, and carry our helmets into the meeting room. Excitement was through the roof as we waited to hear what Woody had to say, because this is where Woody would hand out Buckeye leaves. If you'd done something significant to positively impact the course of the game, you'd get a leaf—a small circular sticker emblazoned with a five-pointed leaf from a buckeye tree. Woody would announce which players had earned leaves that week, then he'd peel the sticker off the sheet and apply it to our helmet himself. It was better than Christmas.

Recognition was one of Woody's strengths. When he was tough on you, he was tough. Yet if that's all he had been, he'd have lost the team. He knew better. These days, you see all kinds of teams with stickers on their helmets, but Woody pioneered that tradition.

This was the first experience where I truly understood the impact that ceremony and recognition have on individual players in a team sport. True team players are winners only if the team wins. They do not seek, nor even necessarily want, individual recognition. But if that recognition comes because the player's performance helped the team win, then that is the ultimate prize.

The stickers also had an impact outside the locker room. They sent a silent message of achievement to fans and the public. In many ways, Buckeye leaves are not unlike the "19,341 ft" sticker that someone might display to show they've climbed Mount Kilimanjaro, or the pink Cadillac awarded to the highest earner for Mary Kay. These things are powerful because they've been earned. A Christian may display a fish symbol or an NRA member a logo sticker, but all they're saying is that they are part of a group. They have not necessarily achieved anything.

Buckeye leaves were something different. We died for those stickers. That kind of recognition from Woody and from your teammates for doing something that helped to win a game was as good as it got. Back then, I'd have taken a Buckeye leaf over a million dollars or any other award, and everyone else felt the same. After the week's awards, we'd sit around looking at everyone's helmets, counting leaves to see who had the most. It brought the team together each week, and the pride that Woody showed in us as a group and in each individual—well, that's how championships are made.

But I'd have a long way to go before I ever felt that kind of glory. As it was, my freshman year got off to a rocky start in pretty much every way you could imagine.

CHAPTER 4

A Rocky Start

When you've had some success, however small, and you've gotten some steam under you, it's natural to think that momentum will continue. The feeling I had was not cockiness but confidence. I had every reason to believe the same mindset, preparation, commitment, and hard work I applied in the past, which had gotten me where I was, would produce similar results going forward.

It was the start of my freshman season. We'd completed the mile, and for the past four weeks in training camp, I practiced with over a hundred teammates as we prepared for the start of our 1966 campaign. Campus would open soon, bringing with it our first game of the season.

Leading up to that point, it was football twenty-four seven. Meetings, film study, playbooks, practices, scrimmages, weight training. Every day, I saw the same people and did the same thing on repeat. The only difference was the date on the calendar. As monotonous as it was, I learned that repetition develops actions that are repeatable, even in times when the pressure and stress of the situation are at their greatest level. That was the point—to ensure that, come game time, we'd run in accordance with our programming. That we'd function, essentially, on autopilot, our brains and bodies running a series of algorithms and if-then scenarios so reflexively that they required little to no conscious thought.

In my day, freshmen were ineligible to play in games. Our role was to help the varsity players prepare for next week's opponent. The only vesting we had in the outcome was that losing meant the following week's practice would be unbearable. If we won, practices would still be grueling, but a little less so. So for those first four weeks and on into the season, I poured my all into football.

Steadily, I was beginning to understand the meaning and demands of being an athlete at Ohio State. Yet with the start of the fall quarter came my indoctrination into the meaning of being a student athlete, and for this I was not prepared.

Woody believed his players should be students first and athletes second. As such, our college experience was very much the same as the other forty thousand–plus students. During the school year, we lived in the regular student dorms and ate in the same cafeterias, the exception being dinners during the season, which we ate as a team. In addition, we each carried a full course load, which amounted to somewhere between sixteen and eighteen credits per quarter.

During football season, my schedule was the same all four years at OSU. Classes were scheduled from 8 a.m. until 1 p.m. The demands of football started at 2 p.m. with meetings, weight training, film study, and practice. The days wrapped up with dinner at 7 p.m., then the remainder of the hours before bed were dedicated to study.

During the fall quarter of my freshman year, of the eighteen hours of classes I was taking, five were credited to an entry-level biology class. It was a refresher course for most of my fellow students, reviewing what they'd learned in high school. But for me, most of it was new material.

Every Monday, Wednesday, and Friday, eight hundred students assembled for an 8 a.m. lecture, leaving Tuesdays and Thursdays for labs. Lab study mostly involved the use of microscopes, and while I'd had two years of biology in high school, the fact that we didn't have microscopes came back to haunt me. I struggled to figure out the workings of the equipment. It took two weeks for me to realize that the reason every slide I viewed looked like a curly black line was because what I was actually looking at was my eyelash.

I pulled my first ever all-nighter studying for my first biology midterm. As midnight turned to dawn, I dozed, then woke abruptly and realized I was about to miss the exam. By the time I sprinted across campus to the test site, I was ten minutes late and the door was locked. The professor either took pity on me or tired of my pleading—whatever the reason, he relented and allowed me to take the test.

When I entered the room, I saw fifty different stations, each set up with a microscope and a series of slides. We were to analyze each slide, then answer a series of questions. I was led to an open spot to begin. I moved through several stations before I noticed something odd—the students behind me in the rotation seemed rather agitated. My curiosity was satisfied when the professor appeared next to me and informed me that the perspiration I'd been leaving all over the slides was making it impossible for the students following me to clearly view them. Thanks to my sprint to the lab, I was sweating worse than when I'd run the mile.

Not surprisingly, I failed the midterm exam and the entire course. Unfortunately, things weren't looking much better on the field.

In his twenty-eight seasons as head coach, Woody had two losing seasons: 1957 and 1966—my freshman year. We ended the season with a record of 4–5. As I quickly discovered, Buckeye fans only love a winner and will not tolerate a loser. As our losses mounted, the fans became more and more vocal about their displeasure, flying banners over the stadium and chanting, "Goodbye, Woody!" Wearing my letter sweater to class was truly a red badge of courage.

For the first time in my life, I could see, taste, and feel failure. It was right there staring me in the face. Not only was I struggling academically, but it also seemed that Woody and the team were struggling as well.

If Woody was replaced, I would always be branded as his recruit. The new coach would have no commitment to or expectations of me, and possibly no use for my skills. I could be forever relegated to the bench.

Academically, my winter quarter grades would determine if I remained on scholarship and an OSU student, or if I'd be returning home to find my place holding up a parking meter. I fared little better in my other courses, ending the quarter with a GPA of 1.653. Underscoring the magnitude of this failure was the fact that the bar was already set relatively low. Student athletes needed only a 2.0 GPA to stay off probation, and I hadn't even managed that.

There was some relief, however. Soon after the season ended, the powers that be at the school made it very clear that Woody was never in jeopardy of being replaced. One potential for disaster had been averted, yet I still faced my academic reckoning.

I returned for the start of winter quarter on a Sunday evening in mid-January. Tacked to the door of my dorm room was a note instructing me to see Coach Hayes ASAP. I knew he'd be in his office, so I trudged over to the basketball arena, then slogged up the stairs to the second floor. Dead man walking.

His door was open, so I took a deep breath and crossed the threshold.

Woody looked up from his desk and over his steel-rimmed glasses. "Son," he said plainly, "if you have another quarter like the one you just had, you will not be with us any longer." Then he looked back down at his desk. Transmission over, message received.

It was a long, cold walk back to my dorm room. As devastated, embarrassed, and anxious as I felt, Art's words materialized in my brain: "You are still standing, and in the game."

During the winter quarter, the only commitment I had to football was conditioning. Three days a week, for about two and a half hours each day, the coaches would run us through a series of drills designed to ensure we remained relatively fit. They didn't want us starting from scratch come spring.

Now I was engaged in a whole new ball game. I realized that to this point, virtually every skill and tool that had benefited me in athletics no longer applied when it came to academics. I'd gotten to OSU through a combination of commitment, hard work, dedication, and overcoming adversity. Organizing, prioritizing, and time management were not part of the equation. These were all skills I now required, but was severely lacking. The good news was that my pared-down athletic schedule left me with extra free time, slowing the pace of life and affording me a chance to figure things out.

In the fall, I'd assimilated to life as an OSU athlete, and that term, I started to plug in the "student" part of the equation. By the time winter quarter ended, I had earned a 3.455 GPA. Woody himself called to tell me the news before I left for spring break. I think he was even more excited than I was. From that point on, and to my great relief, I was never in academic jeopardy again. On we marched into spring practice.

NCAA rules permitted teams to conduct twenty organized practices during the spring quarter. Coaches used this time as an opportunity to experiment with different plays and systems and to observe the freshmen, who would gain eligibility to play on varsity in the coming season. At the conclusion of the twenty practices, an intersquad scrimmage was held in the stadium. The game was open to the public. During my time at OSU, the "spring game," as it was called, drew as many as forty-five thousand fans, all wanting to glimpse a preview of next year's team. Today, the spring game is televised on ESPN, with upward of ninety thousand fans in the stands.

In my day, it was the first glimpse fans got of us up-and-comers. The spring game was of importance for freshmen and reserve players who were eager to demonstrate to the coaches their capabilities under gamelike conditions. For the veterans, the objective was not to get hurt. Nowadays, promising players are tracked relentlessly starting in high school, and from the moment they're drafted, the world knows their stats. By the time the freshmen step onto the field for the spring game, expectations are already through the roof.

That year, Woody had been using the spring as an opportunity to try out a system for calling plays from the sidelines and shuttling them to the huddle via a player substitution. I was chosen as one of three "messengers," along with a running back and wide receiver. The way the system worked, we messengers would stand next to Woody on the sidelines. He would give the play to one of us, who then ran to the huddle and relayed it to the quarterback.

There were three requirements to be selected as a messenger. You needed to be talented enough to play with the starting unit, fast enough to reach the huddle without receiving a delay-of-game penalty, and have a solid enough memory that you could relay the proper play once you arrived at the huddle.

The only thing Woody hated more than losing was mistakes. Fumbles, interceptions, and missed tackles or blocks would elicit some of his worst tantrums. His outbursts, however, were reserved for the season, when the game had real meaning to it. Or so I thought.

The game was rolling along when suddenly a running back fumbled. Owing to my role as messenger, I was standing next to Woody when it happened. Upon seeing the fumble, in a split second, Woody snatched his wire-rimmed glasses from his face and crushed them in his hands. They were so mangled they looked like our starting center had stomped on them.

Then, just as quickly, he calmly folded his hands behind his back and acted like nothing had happened. An equipment manager observed that Woody's hands were bleeding and offered him a towel. I thought he was going to take the poor kid's head off. Two more messages received: Don't mess up, and don't do anything until you're asked.

At the close of my freshman year, I returned home, battle weary and dazed but undamaged. That's when I first learned that at times success looks different from what we anticipated or wanted it to look like.

In spite of our losing record and my having been on academic probation, I ended the year with a sense of pride and achievement. I knew I had a lot of work in front of me, but I was still in the fight. In any engagement, you may not ultimately win the war, but the battles along the way are still important. Winning when and where you can matters. It means something. You need to stay poised and keep focused, and hang in for a better day.

As I returned home, I felt much like a professional golfer who, during the opening round, faced gale-force winds, sleet and rain, and approaching darkness. He finished his round over par with no birdies, had some awesome saves, and did not compound his mistakes. When you have a tough day, or season, the goal is to keep yourself in contention. Put yourself in a position to succeed in the future, because there are more rounds to play before a winner will be crowned.

Through much of my freshman year, the wind was in my face. It was a tough year mentally and emotionally. As others likely saw it, if I was going to see game time the following year, it would only be on special teams, or at best as a backup. But the only person's opinions and beliefs that were of importance were my own.

Overcoming adversity tests one's character. Overcoming failure tests one's soul. I was fine with adversity, but going forward, I vowed to do absolutely everything in my power to stay as far away as possible from failure. In that first year, I had made some critical saves, and I had salvaged enough to stay in contention. I was battered and bruised, but I was still there, and that meant I had a chance. Come hell or high water, I was going to make the most of it.

CHAPTER 5

Directing My Own Destiny

Fear is bred largely by the unknown. There were no surprises, anxiety attacks, or "Oh shit!" moments as I entered my second training camp. As a sophomore, I knew what was expected of me, along with the performance that was required to achieve the goals I had set for myself. Chief among them was earning enough playing time to be awarded a varsity letter. The day I left home for camp, out of nowhere, my dad said that if I earned a letter, he'd buy me a car. As dazzled as I was by the notion of owning my own set of wheels, I had all the self-motivation I needed to get the job done. A car would be a bonus.

The sun was still fresh in the sky when we assembled for our first day of camp, and the coaches reviewed the drill for the now-familiar routine of the six-minute mile. It was as tough as I remembered, but this time I'd expended enough pain and agony in preparing for the season that I didn't have to generate the same spectacle to get myself across the finish line in time. As Vince Lombardi, former head coach of the Green

Bay Packers, once famously said: "The will to win is not nearly as important as the will to prepare to win."

At the start of camp, I was listed on the depth chart as third-team offensive tackle, a status that neither surprised nor disappointed me. Ahead of me were players who either were veterans or who'd demonstrated more potential than I had during our freshman year. The way I saw it, it wasn't particularly important where I started, only where I finished. Little did I know, my climb up the depth chart was about to commence.

It happened during our first fall scrimmage. I was positioned against a fellow sophomore—a defensive tackle who'd been heavily recruited out of high school. It was expected that he'd be competing for a starting position. On this particular play, my assignment was to block said tackle in any direction I could take him. Then the running back could run through whatever opening I'd created. When the snap came, I executed my block in such a way that the tackle ended up on his back with me on top of him. Embarrassed and flat-out pissed, he could not get off the ground fast enough.

Nothing got by Woody. Having observed the play, he blew his whistle and demanded that the defensive tackle and I return to our positions on the ground. As we lay there, face mask to face mask, Woody directed the entire team to gather around us. "This is how we block at Ohio State!" he exclaimed.

I was simultaneously proud and mortified. Woody's propensity to always embrace a teaching moment had done nothing to bolster my relationship with the defensive tackle. It would be quite a while before he'd even acknowledge my presence. As I recall, he didn't speak to me for at least a year. Yet eventually, as time went on and memories softened, we became good friends.

The payoff for that big play came the next day when I was promoted to second team. Then, one week before our opening game, I was awarded the role of messenger in the play-calling system we'd developed during spring practice.

To be sure, I am a huge proponent of the value of steady progress and hard work. Reliability, consistency, and determination please any coach or leader. But to truly separate yourself from the competition requires bold moves with exceptional results. That's what I'd accomplished with that one block. In just a few potent seconds, I had changed my prospects. And with that, I looked forward to my first time on the field during an Ohio State football game.

Teams, regardless of their pursuit, perform at their highest level when their routine is structured and consistent. This allows for the team to stay focused, concentrating solely on the preparation and execution that's required of them to perform at their best. At Ohio State, there was a structured routine for everything, and I mean *everything*. Every day of the week, the schedule for that day was the same as the prior week. Structure and repetition were especially on display just before a game.

I imagine that the spectators—at least those not among the student body—supposed that on game day, players simply showed up at the appointed time. What they might not have known was that Woody had put into place a series of routines meant to put us in the proper psychological framework for the game, and we adhered to them religiously. We spent all that time and effort preparing physically, but just as important was our mental game. All that work could quickly go out the window if we lost concentration.

The night before every home game, dinner was held at the Ohio State University Golf Club. If it was an away game, the team dinner was held at a local restaurant—the same restaurant each year we traveled to that city. Following dinner, we boarded two buses. The first-team defense and first-team offense rode in the primary bus, and the AYOs—"all you others"—boarded the second. The buses would head to the local theater for a private showing. Each year, an assistant coach had the thankless task of selecting the movie. The only time the movie was not a Western or a war film was when we saw *Easy Rider*. The movie starred Jack Nicholson, Dennis Hopper, and Peter Fonda. They were three hippies with long hair, riding across the country on their motorcycles, high on drugs. At one point, they expressed their disapproval of the Vietnam War by burning the American flag. That set Woody into such a rage, he nearly fired the assistant coach on the spot.

After the movie, it was on to the hotel. At 9 p.m., Woody assembled the team for a thirty-minute film session. Enough entertainment—he wanted to get our minds back on football. While watching the film, he would randomly quiz us about our assignment on a particular play.

When we returned to our rooms, we'd find a cup of hot chocolate, two sugar cookies, and an apple, delivered by the hotel staff. Woody had the notion that it would relax us, and we would sleep better. (It was his belief, however, that the most important night's sleep was not the night before the game, but two nights prior.) At ten o'clock, Woody personally conducted bed check. He wanted to get a sense of our mood and emotions leading up to the game.

The next morning, after our pregame meal, Woody and the two cocaptains—one from the offense and the other from defense—would lead the team on a walk around the hotel grounds to help us digest the food. Back in our rooms, we gathered our belongings, then boarded the buses for the drive to the stadium.

I looked forward to our police escort almost as much as the game itself, always claiming a window seat so as not to miss the spectacle. I'd peer out, entranced, as four motorcycle policemen would redirect traffic in such a way that the buses could maintain a speed of forty-five miles per hour. It was like watching a well-choreographed dance. Without fail, we would leave the hotel and arrive at the field with no more than a minute's travel time between them, all thanks to those policemen.

Once inside the stadium locker room, we were taped as needed, reviewed the game plan with our respective coaches, and got dressed. We then assembled at the entrance to the tunnel that led onto the field.

The very first time I stood at the end of that tunnel, I was enveloped in a paradoxical experience. My emotions were high. I was an emotional player anyway, and those moments of anticipation dialed up the intensity even further. At the same time, a kind of numbness descended upon me like a fog. I was devoid of thought, suspended in a kind of Twilight Zone with no immediate understanding of what was about to happen. Combined with a lack of physical sensation, it made for an out-of-body experience. I couldn't place myself in the moment. It was like I was an observer—an anthropologist or an alien, taking in a scene that was totally foreign to me. Some part of me could hear the roar of the stadium, but internally, my mind was silent.

Eventually, it was time to roll, and I followed my teammates out onto the field. As I was standing there, surrounded by the throngs, it was as if someone had picked up the remote control and was steadily turning the volume louder, then louder. Seventy-three thousand fans, clad in scarlet and gray, revved up and ready to cheer or jeer us as our performance warranted. The largest crowd I had played for in high school numbered twenty-five hundred.

I grasped for focus by attempting to review my assignment, only to find that I couldn't remember a thing. Not the plays, the techniques . . . nothing. I knew I was there for a reason and that I had a specific role, but the fundamentals of the task at hand escaped me. I reasoned that if I got moving, it would start coming back to me, but all throughout warm-ups, the cloud continued.

As the offensive line was warming up, I looked up and saw a familiar figure standing on the track about twenty-five feet away. It was my father. We made eye contact. He didn't wave or smile, and neither did I. To this day, I have no idea how he got permission to be down on the track, but there he was. At first, I was elated to see him, but my joy was quickly followed by terror. I knew he was going to be there that day watching from the stands, but in that moment, seeing him, the full magnitude of what I was about to experience landed inside me like a car crash.

My father died in 1997. A short time later, my mother re-called for me a conversation she and my father had had back in my Ohio State days. They were in the stands, watching my first game, and my dad turned to her. "Did you ever think we'd be sitting here watching our son play for Ohio State?" That was all he said, and her relaying it to me was a gift. I knew all along that my father was proud of me, but this was special. It was the closest thing to a "Way to go!" I ever got from him. It was posthumous, but it was mine.

When my mother shared that story, it struck me that there's value not only in succeeding in something but also in having someone to share it with. In fact, the latter can be so meaningful as to actually overshadow the achievement itself. It's about how much someone else's appreciation means to you, and the things that don't always need to be said.

When the pregame warm-up concluded, the team re-turned to the locker room, then went back onto the field. Bits and pieces floated by, but there was no clarity. Then, I be-came vaguely aware that someone was singing a song I rec-ognized. . . . It was the national anthem. I was always nervous and hyped up before a game. But once I took the field and the first contact was made, I could hear no crowd noise, no band; I only heard the sound of the quarterback's voice and saw the face of my opponent across from me.

As the game wore on, thankfully my senses returned. Like my nerves over the first six-minute mile, that first game was the only time I experienced that kind of overwhelm. I got excited—to say the least—before each game, but I never again lost my wits. I never felt totally comfortable during the game, but I unfroze.

When I took the field for the first time, my head was spinning. Woody had given me the play, and off to the huddle I sprinted. I leaned in, but as I began to relay the play to the quarterback, my mind went blank. I had gone brain-dead and could not for the life of me remember what Woody had said. Realizing I had nothing to convey to him, our quarterback called his own play. Fortunately, the result went in our favor, but when I returned to the sidelines, Woody was waiting for me. He asked me what happened to the play he called. Terrified, recalling those glasses he'd crushed, I replied that the quarterback changed the play by audibling at the line of scrimmage. Woody thought for a second, then said, "Goddamn, that is smart football!"

Disaster was averted, but only for a moment. Unfortunately, my overwhelm continued, and I turned in a poor performance. We ended the game as winners, yet I felt anything but. After every one of my games, I could recall every play with photographic accuracy. On this day, that talent felt like a curse. My recollections of the game were confirmed the next day when the offensive line met with our coach to review the film.

My line coach was one of the best in the country. In his eight years at Ohio State, he developed seven All-American offensive linemen. After three hours of critiquing each play over and over, I was certain I would at best be demoted as a messenger and relegated to the bench. Finally, the torture session ended, and we gathered our things to leave. As I was about to exit, I heard the coach call out: "Hutch! Come on back here." I thought he was going to demote me now rather than wait until the next day's practice.

"Let's go over the tape again," he said. This time, as we watched each play, he went into great detail, identifying what had gone wrong that prevented me from executing my assignment. His analysis revealed that my poor performance was caused by a lack of concentration, focus, and poise. All these things *I* caused, not my opponent. In other words, I hadn't been beaten or outplayed; I'd lost. It was my own fault, plain and simple.

There are no excuses for losses that could have been prevented, nor is there shame in being dominated by someone who, on that day, was superior. It's the same in the business world. If you've just given a sales presentation and you've done everything as well as possible but you don't get the result you wanted, then it just wasn't meant to be. Yet more often than not, that's not the case. Typically, what happens is that we defeat ourselves. We don't prepare enough, or we don't execute well. The reality is that we have a tremendous ability to control our outcomes by what we do, regardless of what someone else does or doesn't do. But it's easy to point the finger. It's easy to say, for instance, that someone else's behavior put you in a bad mood. The reality is that you put yourself in that frame of mind through your reaction to the stimulus they provided. It wasn't what happened, but how you reacted to it.

Well, on that day, I got lucky, and the result of my lackluster performance did not spell the end of my season. Through fortune or just the confidence of my coaches, I was given a second chance, and I did well enough the following week to remain in the rotation for the remainder of the season. In the end, I accumulated enough playing time to earn a varsity jacket.

The jacket came in handy during the Ohio winters, but not

in the early fall. The body of the jacket was heavy wool, and the sleeves were leather. Though the temperature was in the seventies when I got it, I persisted in wearing it. I was sweating worse than I had during my freshman biology midterm, but I did not care.

When I returned home, it was time for Dad to make good on his promise of a car. Apparently, there was some misunderstanding over whether he meant a new car or simply a car. This was my first lesson in getting things in writing. The upshot was that I was presented with the keys to a 1955 Pontiac Bonneville. It was a tank, but it was my tank.

I'd spent the bulk of my freshman year adjusting to circumstances and situations for which I had little experience. During my sophomore year, I learned that my outcomes were dependent on what I did, not what was done to me.

As I looked forward to my junior year, I was optimistic. We were coming off a 6–3 record, a very talented freshman class was about to join the varsity, and thanks to a graduating player, a starting tackle position had opened up. Life was good, and so were my prospects.

CHAPTER 6

A Disappointed Champion

When we got to full practice in the fall of my junior year, the coaches made the decision to move our starting tight end to the offensive tackle position, which relegated me to second team. There was a glimmer of hope, because the player in question had failed to complete the mile in under six minutes while I had finished it in the required time. Maybe, I'd thought, Woody would be disappointed in his performance and demote him and elevate me.

As promised, the tackle ran the mile again every day at 5:30 a.m. This went on for six days, until one morning, he reported to the track under a heavy fog. Visibility was less than six or seven feet. As he was chugging to the line to complete his first lap, the assistant coach who was timing him called out, "I can't see you." The player completed the second lap on pace to fail again, at which point the coach declared more vehemently, "I can't see you." On the third lap, with the player's pace dwindling even more, the coach was in desperation mode. "I can't see you!" he screamed one last time. Finally, the player understood what the coach was trying to tell him. Miraculously, he somehow emerged from the fog and finished in the required time. No one knows how much distance he cut off, but the assistant coach could honestly report to Woody that the player had crossed the line in under six minutes.

My hope of being handed the starting position was quickly snuffed out. During our team meeting the night of the tackle's successful mile, Coach Hayes singled him out for his determination and commitment. "That's what it is going to take for us to win a national championship!" he declared. Knowing the real story, the team could hardly contain itself. Woody never missed an opportunity to motivate and inspire, even if the details were a little foggy.

Of course, I would later realize that Woody knew exactly what had happened. The thing is, there's a point where every good leader has to say "Enough's enough" and move on. Under certain circumstances, the ground rules you set have to become flexible, or they become a negative more than a positive. If that player had been forced to continue lining up early every morning and running to exhaustion, eventually it would have diminished his ability to perform on the field. That would have hurt the team. There was no sense in that, and the fog gave Woody a perfect out.

The previous spring, I'd been vying for that open spot with a classmate. The way I saw it, you couldn't have a better setup than that. All through spring practice, we alternated in the position, and left with neither one of us being declared the next season's starter. When I'd returned home for the summer before my junior year, three words were imprinted in my mind: Best man wins.

But as we were to learn, the coaches had other plans. Once the new tackle was slotted into that position and had completed the mile, unless he screwed up royally, that was the end of the story for me and my classmate. Now we had bookend tackles who were each six foot five and 265 pounds. In the end, both went on to become All-Americans, then first-round NFL draft choices. To give a sense of how good these guys were, it's nearly unheard of for two players in the same position from the same school to go in the first round of the NFL draft. Clearly, it was the right choice for the coaches to make, but needless to say, I was extremely disappointed. Suddenly, it was looking like I'd actually see less field time than I had my sophomore season.

As it turned out, I did end up playing in the first three games because the tackle sprained his ankle, but once he was healthy, he was back in, and I was out. Other than special teams, I didn't see the light of day, and that made for an exceptionally long year. But I wasn't bitter. I couldn't do anything about it, and it would have been selfish to think "Poor me." That's what it means to be on a team—to recognize when what serves the group needs to supersede your personal goals and what you want for yourself.

I've found that in general, when you're disappointed, you can go one of two ways. The first is that you can let it affect your attitude and your play. That will leave a bad taste in the coaches' mouths and essentially make it a no-brainer for them to let you go. When I saw the writing on the wall and it said I wasn't going to see any real playing time that season, I could have shot myself in the foot right there. Instead, I went the other way. I still practiced hard, as though I was going to play. I made the most of the situation that I could make of it. Sometimes, you can do absolutely everything in your ability to make something happen, but then a force outside your control takes over, and you're essentially powerless to create change. In those situations, the only positive thing you can do is to place yourself squarely in front of the door of opportunity so that, should it open, you're ready to walk through.

In my career, I've counseled others who were demoted or who were disappointed when, for whatever reason, they experienced a setback, and I've told them exactly the same thing: Don't ever flunk yourself out. You can either confirm to the powers that be that they made the right decision, or you can bust your ass and make it hard for them to justify their choice. If it doesn't work out in the near term—meaning you're still stuck in the back seat—in the long run, they'll most likely appreciate your attitude and how you handled the situation. Displaying that kind of character, maturity, and patience leaves a good impression going forward, and they're likely to think of you should an opportunity arise. If you do the work, you'll never second-guess the results.

For me, there was also the consolation of looking forward to my senior season. The following year, both those tackles would be gone. When I scanned the depth chart, I knew that, given the variables, there was no one who could keep me off that field. At least, that's what I told myself, and that's what propelled me through. At the same time, somewhere in my subconscious lived a kernel of uncertainty—a seed of anxiety that was threatening to germinate.

As it turned out, in spite of my lack of playing time, my junior year was magical. We went undefeated, and on the way, we trounced our biggest rival. The Michigan game ended with a score of 50–14. If that score alone wasn't enough to fuel Michigan's desire for revenge, Woody's coaching decision at the end of the game surely would be.

As the seconds ticked off, we scored another touchdown. Instead of kicking for the extra point, Woody called for a two-point conversion. At the postgame press conference, when reporters asked Woody why he'd opted to go for two, he said, simply, "Because I could not go for three." Michigan would have an entire season to build up their ire over that one. In the meantime, it was on to the Rose Bowl, where we faced the University of Southern California; we were ranked one and two, respectively. It was the experience of a lifetime and a situation every college player dreams of.

Ironically, the year before, I'd been lying on the family room floor, watching Indiana play in the Rose Bowl. My mother asked me, "Don't you wish you'd gone to Indiana?"

"No," I said, without missing a beat, "because I'm going to the Rose Bowl with Ohio State." Check.

Yet while we'd filled our heads with California dreams, we had a rude awakening on our chartered flight to Pasadena. At one point midflight, one of the trainers tapped me on the back. "We're ready for you," he said and motioned me toward the back of the plane. There, the trainers had set up two taping stations. Woody wanted us to be ready to practice the moment we were wheels down. On the tarmac awaiting our arrival were the mayor of Pasadena, the Rose Queen, her court, and what seemed like every media outlet imaginable—it was the full red-carpet treatment. But instead of enjoying the attention, once we deplaned, we walked straight to the awaiting buses, and off we went to practice. This was a business trip.

On the surface, that might not seem like a big thing—to be called back midflight to get taped. And for other players, perhaps it wasn't. But it impacted me deeply in terms of my mindset going forward. Sure, Woody's rituals and routines were designed to get us in the proper headspace to play. That I understood. Yet somehow, this triggered something inside me—an insight I would employ throughout the next four decades of work.

I've done a lot of business travel over the years, which is perhaps the world's greatest understatement. By the end of my career, there were entire stretches of time when I'd essentially lived on the road. At times, I traveled with others, and I saw how we approached our excursions differently.

When you work in an office or some other routine setting, it's easy to stay in business mode. After all, your environment doesn't change. When you travel, that's a different experience, so you need to employ a different mindset. Gone are your everyday in-office routines. How you travel, when you travel, what you do when you travel, unless you've got someone else choreographing it for you—it's all an open book. You have the latitude to make that experience look like anything you want it to be—within your budgetary constraints, of course.

When I was in the NFL, over the seasons, we'd go to the same cities multiple times, so you got to know what they had on offer outside the stadium. As we approached an away game, other players would spend part of their downtime planning what they wanted to do when they got there, whether it was seeing friends or family, going to certain restaurants, and so on. I did that, too, but it was always secondary to planning what I was going to do to further my business purpose on that trip. I always started with one question: How can I be as effective and efficient on this trip as possible? I instituted personal routines to help me stay focused. Sure, if I had extra time, I'd do whatever it was I wanted to do beyond business. But in the NFL and beyond, it was always business first, pleasure second.

When I was a regional manager, traveling to multiple cities each week, I'd focus on getting the most done in the least amount of time. I was based in a location where I could get direct flights to anywhere I needed to go. The earliest flights left around six thirty or seven in the morning, which meant I was up and getting ready at four or four thirty. My goal was always to get to my destination in time for the opening of business in that town, whatever the time zone. I had the latitude to fly at any time during the day I wanted to. I could have spent more time and more money traveling, and no one would have questioned it, but that was contrary to my personal aim. I'd arrive in the city that morning ready to work, sometimes flying to the next city that very night so I'd be there for the opening of their workday.

The mentality is about asking yourself, "What's the objective here? What am I trying to accomplish?" and focusing on that. That seems straightforward, and it is. Yet how many people do you know who actually do that? As a result of not doing so, we can lose focus, becoming less efficient and effective. I'm not saying you have to drive hard all the time. In fact, one of the benefits of efficiency is that you get to enjoy your time off. You're not flying back home on a Saturday, cutting into your weekend, because you didn't want to take that 6 a.m. flight earlier in the week.

Heading to the Rose Bowl, when our plane went wheels down, we knew what we were there for. That said, we were allowed to enjoy a visit to Disneyland, as guests of the park, for half a day. We were even honored with a parade down Main Street, USA, featuring all the Disney characters. At one point, the entire offensive line decided to ride the Pirates of the Caribbean ride. It had to be the most weight that poor boat had ever carried—easily over two thousand pounds of humanity all piled in. All went well until we sped down a hill into a pool of water and the boat derailed.

There we were, stuck in a tunnel, staring at a lit-up scene of pirates incessantly singing "Yo ho, yo ho, the pirate's life for me!" We were prisoners of the buccaneers for more than twenty minutes before we were mercifully rescued. By then, the song was emblazoned in our brains, and we continued to sing it as we exited the ride. On the other side of the fence, throngs of parkgoers had amassed, waiting to board. Imagine their amusement when a boatload of meatheads—the entire Buckeye offensive line—appeared, all singing the pirate song at the top of our lungs. It was such a sight they asked us to stop and pose for photos.

That wasn't the only unusual incident of the trip. Each year, the Rose Bowl committee hosted a luncheon at the Hollywood Palladium. It was a big affair, with the USC players seated on one side, while we were on the other. Before the event started, we were all standing outside, waiting to enter the backstage area, when this guy—who knows how he got in there—came up to me and said, "Are you Chuck Hutchison from Carrollton, Ohio?"

I looked at him, confused as to who he could possibly be. "Yes, sir, I am," I said.

He smiled and started telling me how he was a traveling salesman whose route took him across Ohio every month or two. "Each time I go through Carrollton, I stop at Coley's Stag," he said. Yes, *that* Coley's, of parking-meter fame—or rather, infamy. Most of us just called it Coley's, but the fact was that ever since Russ and Henry Cole had opened the tavern in the 1930s, it served only men. I think it stayed that way through the 1980s, or perhaps even the '90s. Russ and Henry looked as antiquated as their no-women policy, as if they'd walked straight out of the 1800s with their long, fluffy white beards.

Coley's was a real dive, but it was our dive. If anyone was visiting home from out of town or you wanted to catch up with someone, you knew there was a good chance you could find them at Coley's. The place was run-down, the floorboards were uneven, and some of the barstools were shaky. All of us knew where to walk and where to sit to avoid the wobbles. In the back room were three pool tables. I can't tell you how many out-of-towners were hustled by locals at those tables. It wasn't that the locals were so good; it was that the tables weren't level, and those who played them regularly knew exactly how the balls would roll.

Everything at Coley's was homemade, from the burgers to the buns. On any day of the week, at any time of day, there would be two big pots sitting on the stove, one of which was bean soup and the other chili. I don't think those pots ever saw the sink or a good washing. When the levels got low, they'd simply add more ingredients. The lower the chili was, the spicier it got. You could walk in and ask Russ or Henry, "How low's the chili?" and depending on their answer, you could determine if perhaps you were better off with the bean soup. At Coley's, $2.50 would get you a ladle of either, which perfectly filled their ceramic bowls, a sandwich, and a mug of draft beer—usually Black Label or Old Dutch, a beer made in Pennsylvania.

The next time I went home to visit, I went over to Coley's and showed them the card the salesman had given me. "Oh yeah," they said, "that guy comes through here every month or two." They even remembered his regular order. To this day, I have no idea what he was doing in Pasadena, but they must have been talking about me at Coley's because otherwise, I don't know how he'd have known about me. Now that I was on a championship team, it seemed that the tenor of the town gossip, and my presumed prospects, had changed.

The night before the Rose Bowl, Woody deviated slightly from our typical pregame routine. He worried that we'd be hassled by friends and family reaching out to us for last-minute tickets, distracting us from our mission. Instead of spending the night at the hotel, he moved us all to a monastery in the hills overlooking Los Angeles. Each of us had our own monk cell—a single room with no lock on the door, a small desk containing a Bible, a lamp, a chair, a single bed, and a small half bath. "Sparse" was one word for it.

A projector was brought into a common room, and we watched a war movie. The place was downright eerie, and as it turned out, none of us was able to get any sleep. Woody wasn't concerned, though, because of his theory that the sleep you got two nights before was more important. To this day, if I know my schedule will necessitate a night of interrupted sleep, I always try my best to get a good night's rest two nights prior.

Finally, it was game time. We played a solid first half. That was, until just over two minutes before halftime. With the score 10–0 in our favor, USC's running back—a guy named OJ Simpson—hustled eighty yards for a touchdown. As we broke for halftime, the score was tied 10–10.

When Woody entered the locker room, he was furious. "Where's Lou?" he yelled, over and over. He was looking for our defensive back coach, Lou Holtz, because he thought one of our backs should have prevented Simpson from scoring. When he finally located Lou, he roared. "Why did OJ go eighty-five yards for a score?" he demanded.

Not missing a beat, Lou replied, "Because that's all the farther he had to run." From anyone else, Woody might not have tolerated that dose of sarcasm. But it was almost certainly payback for a little Woody-style lesson the head coach had taught Lou earlier in the season, soon after he was hired.

Lou had been a very successful high school coach, and this was his first college position. It was trial by fire, to be sure. One of Woody's major pet peeves was when players stood around with their hands on their hips, or when coaches put their hands in their pockets. He believed that it communicated a sense of defeat or a lack of interest, neither of which was all right with him.

At some point during Lou's first practice, he was standing behind the defense with his hands in his back pockets. The next day, he opened his locker to find that the pockets of all his pants had been sewn shut, a task for which Woody had enlisted the equipment manager. After that, Lou waited for his moment.

Standing there in the locker room at the Rose Bowl, Lou's matter-of-fact response did the near impossible—it rendered Woody speechless. He left the room. After composing himself, he returned and began making adjustments for the second half.

It all came together, and in a glorious finish, we won the game 27–16. We were the 1968 national champions. It was almost more than I could absorb.

Yet as proud as I was to be a member of our 1968 championship team, I was deeply disappointed in my role. I felt as though, on the whole, I had contributed very little to the team's success, and I did not enjoy feeling like a spectator. Still, there was some solace in having added to the effort in some way, however small. These days, when I think about that season, I'm reminded of the movie *Patton* starring George C. Scott as the famous general. In the intro to the movie, Scott is on a stage with the American flag behind him. He's giving his speech to a bunch of troops, reassuring them that it's normal to get confused or disoriented in combat. People often imagine themselves as heroes, but when it comes down to it, war is a messy business. The takeaway was that regardless, they should be proud of themselves for serving their country. "Thirty years from now, when you're sitting around your fireside with your grandson on your knee and he asks you, 'What did you do in the great World War II,' you won't have to say, 'Well . . . I shoveled shit in Louisiana.'"

That pretty much summed up how I characterized my junior year. I hadn't contributed as much as I wanted to, but I wasn't shoveling shit in Louisiana. I think we can all have those experiences in different ways, where even if you didn't play the role you wanted to toward an overall success, you can still be proud of yourself because you were a part of it. You could have been on a losing team, or just sitting at home.

Still, the fact remained that I had one last opportunity to write my legacy at Ohio State, and I was determined not to waste it. With the departure of both our tackles for the NFL, it was now certain that the other junior and I were going to fill those slots. What was uncertain was how we were going to perform. Neither of us was what you'd call a proven commodity. That was how the sports writers framed it, too. Going in to defend our national championship, the Buckeyes would be loaded with experienced seniors and All-Americans—the two exceptions being me and the other guy. I was not going to be the weak link on the team. I did a lot of thinking on the flight home from the Rose Bowl.

I saw myself as a shoo-in for the position my senior year, believing that the only reason the other guy had gotten it the past season was because he was just better. But was that really the case, or could I have done more? That was still a question mark in my mind. There were seven tackles for two open positions. I had the most experience, but as I'd learned at the start of that season, anything could happen. I could get hurt. Or the coaches could decide to invest in a younger player to get them the experience. The thing is, you can't take anything for granted. You can live with surprises if you've done everything you can do to prevent them. I needed to think of everything I could possibly do to prepare so as not to leave anything that was within my control to chance. I needed to leave no doubt.

Traditionally, OSU offensive tackles had always been big, strong, powerful run blockers. It was a profile that suited Woody's offensive strategy of "three yards and a cloud of dust." To that point, I'd done everything I could to emulate the tackles who'd come before me. But as hard as I'd worked, I was not dominating. I had bulk but lacked the strength to accompany it.

When you plateau, if you want to improve, something has to change. You can get strong doing three sets of ten reps, but eventually, you'll stop seeing results. Sure, you can simply add more weight or reps, but if you want big results, sometimes an even bigger change is required. Sometimes, you have to take it down to the studs and build back up again. That was what

I decided to do. Dramatic improvement required dramatic change.

When your body gets used to something, it expends as little energy as possible to do it—hence the plateau. The same thing is true of your brain. The good and bad news about getting good at something is that it becomes easy. That might feel pleasurable, but it means you're no longer improving. So go ahead and enjoy the smooth sailing for about five minutes, then devise your next plan. That is, if you want to keep growing. Some people are fine coasting, or at least that's what they tell themselves. Personally, I have a hard time imagining I'd find that kind of life engaging. For instance, right now, I know a group of retired men. Every day, these guys get up at the same time, they have breakfast—probably the same bowl of corn-flakes or the same scrambled eggs—then meet up for a round of golf. Same tee time every day. When they finish up, they go back to the clubhouse for lunch, play cards in the afternoon, then it's home for dinner and off to bed. The next day, they hit repeat, just like *Groundhog Day*. Maybe on some level, they actually enjoy the routine, but quite frankly, to me it sounds like an expensive brand of torture. I might be alive, technically, but I'd feel like my life was over. And in many ways, it would be. If you want to keep living, you must keep changing. You must keep challenging yourself and stay curious.

There's an adage in college football: "If you're going to have one good year, make it your last one." It wouldn't be my only good year—during my sophomore year, I'd earned my letter, and now I had a championship ring to go with it—but it would definitely be my last shot to make my mark. To some extent, my senior-year strategy was a risk, but it was one that to me was worth the potential reward. And if my final year was a bust, it would be because of decisions I made, not choices or circumstances that had been foisted upon me.

All the way back to Ohio from California, I stared out the

airplane window. But I wasn't taking in the view; I was deep in thought, considering my own attributes and how I might do things differently. If I was going to break out of the mold, what could that look like? The graduating tackles were a lot stronger, but I was quicker. Their game was size and strength and physicality, and mine was rooted in quickness, finesse, and technique. I hadn't beaten them at their game, but what would it look like if I doubled down on mine? How much stronger could my strengths become if I lost weight and developed my speed and agility to their utmost?

That summer, in addition to focusing on losing weight, I incorporated agility drills into my training to improve my lateral movement. I also changed my stance so I could be more explosive when the ball was snapped. But perhaps the biggest help came from my summer job.

In the ten weeks I had before fall practice would begin, I worked for a company that was installing a gas pipeline in my area. For six days a week, twelve hours a shift, I manned a shovel, spending all day cleaning out ditches eight feet deep. My lunch consisted of a sandwich, fruit, and a half gallon of unsweetened iced tea. Then, following work, I would return home, flip on the lights in the backyard, and work through my conditioning program.

By the end of that summer, I had dropped from 260 pounds to a lean, mean 228. I was in the best shape possible. As fall approached, I headed back to campus, where I was about to see if my risk would pay off.

CHAPTER 7

Make or Break

When I reported to camp my senior year, it was like an extreme makeover from the player I was the year before. I'd been above average on most skills across the board, but in the league I was playing in, that made me only pretty okay. And pretty okay doesn't make you a starter. I'd taken a gamble, sacrificing size and betting that I could make my strengths—like being quick off the ball—even stronger. That it would make me a standout. I figured I had a better chance at that than trying to focus on improving my weaknesses. Instead, I was going to live or die by what I did best.

That first day, when I reported for camp, we lined up for the mile as usual. I ran it in five minutes, ten seconds—a blistering time for a tackle. The coaches were stunned. They were impressed, too. It was evident to all that I was working hard to make the most of my last shot. It was an excellent start and got me excited for the season. Still, I knew there was no room to relax. For better or worse, fear of failure has always been more of a driver for me than the thrill of succeeding. That image of the parking meters was never far from my mind.

Fortunately, Woody's vision for the team lined up nicely with what I was bringing to the table. We'd increased the tempo of our offense, meaning that speed and agility were not just a luxury but a necessity. Woody devised a system to call all our offensive plays at the line of scrimmage, and we were among the first teams to develop that capability. Previously, during a typical game, the number of plays we'd run was somewhere in the sixties. Our new approach put us in the seventies. If you're going to run fifteen to twenty more plays during a game, your team needs to be in shape, and we had the athletes capable of executing that approach. As frustrated as I'd been the previous season, during my senior year, things lined up perfectly—not just for me but for the team.

From the start of camp, as an offense, we were really clicking, and as a result, we were confident. Yet in true Woody fashion, he made sure we didn't feel too confident. He consistently drilled into us the sense that unless each player was about to have the best game of his life, we would surely lose.

Still, I was having a good camp. The local sports writers were featuring my progress in their columns, and the coaches were commenting on my improvement and performance.

At the time, the Big Ten sports writers would travel around and observe the teams. Not only did they report on us, but they were also responsible for selecting the all-star squads, All-Americans, and other postseason honors. To put it mildly, their attendance was a big deal.

All eyes were on us during our preseason scrimmage, just two weeks ahead of our last visit home before the season opener. It was our final tune-up for the season and an opportunity for the writers to get a good look at us. I knew I was under consideration for postseason recognition, and I certainly gave them something to look at, but not the way I'd hoped.

Midway through the scrimmage, I went brain-dead and jumped offsides. Not just once, but twice. In a row. The first time, I translated the call into the wrong snap count. Then, I was just too anxious.

After the second time, Woody marched up to me. Wisely, the rest of the offensive unit backed away. Now, Woody was about five foot nine, but what he lacked in stature, he made up for in outrage. He reached up and grabbed my face mask and yanked my head down to his. "Son, you're the dumbest son of a bitch I've ever coached," he growled. "You're the dumbest goddamn player in the Big Ten! Take that jersey off! You don't deserve to wear an Ohio State jersey."

A jersey doesn't just slip off over your pads—it takes some effort. I struggled for a few embarrassingly long moments, while everyone looked on uncomfortably. There was no way anyone was going to step forward to help me. Finally, I wrestled it off. I placed the jersey on the ground, then looked at Woody. "Go in," he barked. I turned and started jogging toward the locker room. I was about a hundred yards from cover when I heard the shrill tweet of Woody's whistle. "Walk!" he ordered, maximizing my humiliation.

Once inside the locker room, I unleashed a storm. I threw absolutely everything I could get my hands on—towels, my helmet, benches. If it could be hoisted, it was airborne. When I finally exhausted myself, I undressed and took a shower. When I came out, the team was coming in. The manager came straight for me. "Woody wants to see you in his office."

Unlike the time I had to go and see Woody about my poor grades, when I was filled with contrition, this time I was furious.

"You know why I did that?" Woody asked.

"No, sir," I said through clenched teeth.

"I did that to make you mad. Are you mad?"

"Oh yes, sir," I affirmed through clenched teeth. "I'm *very* mad. I'm about as mad as I've ever been in my entire life."

Woody nodded. "Good. You play better football when you're mad. I expect you to have a great year. Now get the hell out of my office."

Woody knew he could drive me any way he wanted to, and I wasn't going to quit. That it would push me to be way better than I ever thought I could be on my own. That was Woody's greatest gift—bringing out talent in people they didn't even know they had. His timing was impeccable. I played the rest of that season like a man possessed.

Woody knew each player well, including the best way to motivate us. That was apparent to me almost from the beginning. Some players he'd reprimand in front of the entire team, others he'd dismantle in private, while with others he wouldn't even raise his voice. At first, I thought he was playing favorites, taking it easier on some. But then I realized the method at work. I learned there's a difference between treating everyone equally and treating them the same. You can look at what's happening and think *He's avoiding that guy because that player's got a temper* or *He's not raising his voice to that guy because he's friends with the guy's dad.* In actuality, Woody recognized each player's level of tolerance and acceptance. He expected the same degree of perfection from all of us, but knew how to interact with us in a way that would make us achieve our best results.

At the end of the scrimmage, Woody assembled us and delivered his standard "No babies!" speech. Once we returned from break, it was off to the races, and I had my starting position.

As it turned out, the only time we were truly challenged my senior season was against Illinois. Our quarterback got knocked out, but then our backup came in and saved us. I started every game that season, but other than the Illinois game, I never finished one, because by the time we reached the fourth quarter, it was all wrapped up.

That set us up perfectly for what would be the most important game of the season, against our biggest rival—Michigan. The matchup was just as significant as the previous year's Rose Bowl, because if we won, we would secure both the national championship and the Big Ten titles. But my hopes for a magical year were not meant to be.

Going in, Michigan had a 7–2 record, and we were seventeen-point favorites, but we sure didn't look like it on the field. During the second half, we threw five interceptions. We lost 24–12. Our twenty-two-game winning streak was broken, and our hopes for a second championship were dashed. And Michigan got their payback. To be fair, I do believe that Michigan won that game fairly. I'm sure I could manufacture any number of excuses for our performance, but the fact is we came in strong. We had a great week of practice, and in spite of the odds, we weren't overconfident. It just happened to be their day. We made mistakes during that game, and Michigan was able to capitalize on them. Sports writers called it one of the greatest upsets in college football.

The way the rules were set up, because we'd gone to the Rose Bowl the year before, we weren't eligible to go that year, so our season was over. I don't think there are words to even describe the disappointment I felt. It's easier for me now to acknowledge that Michigan deserved to win. We were the better team on paper, but that's not how you determine winners and losers. They had placed themselves squarely in front of that door of opportunity, and each time we opened it, they marched right through.

That game left more of an impression on me than any other game I played in my life. The stakes were high, and we failed. Recovering from an outcome as devastating as that took a lot of time, reflection, and soul-searching. It's not an exaggeration to say that to this day, roughly six decades later, I am still unpacking its lessons. Yet as they say, you learn from failure more than you learn from success, but it doesn't happen naturally. Insight is not a natural by-product of loss—you must actively seek out the lessons. I've deconstructed that game over and over these past many years, and while, quite frankly, the loss still stings, I recognize that I have gained a significant amount from it.

That game helped me understand that a well-lived life is, in large measure, about handling unexpected outcomes with dignity, acceptance, and grace. I realized that no single game or experience could ever make me a winner or a loser, an expert or uninformed, superior or inferior. In the end, doing my best is worth much more than being the best. I learned how to hold my head up and get something good out of a situation even when the outcome isn't what I wanted. As the saying goes: "You win some, you lose some, some are rained out, but you've got to dress for them all."

I also learned that the more you have on the line when things don't go your way, the better it sets you up for things that go beyond just dealing with adversity. When it really comes hard, the results may not be great, but the effort you had to put in to generate them actually moves you forward. It's not victory itself that progresses you; it's the work you put into it, win or lose.

That's what the Michigan game did for me. As gut-wrenching as it was, it gave me a coat of armor of sorts. It's not that future losses or failures wouldn't bother me. It's that having had such a hard experience, you then know how you'll react when something that painful happens again. You'll know how you're going to respond to it. That's no longer a question mark. And that distinguishes you.

Everyone can handle things when they're going well. It's

the round where nothing's going your way—when you can't get a putt to drop to save your life. Still, it could be the best round you've ever played. The final tally may show you as one over par, but you still grew as a player. Sometimes, your best performance isn't reflected in the results.

As a coach or a manager, you're looking for the people who, when something goes wrong, look to themselves and what they personally could have done better, rather than pointing fingers. The people who want to offload it on someone else are the ones I can't get rid of fast enough. After that Michigan game, every single player flew home thinking about what they did to contribute to our loss. Even Woody blamed himself when we lost, for not getting us prepared enough. (But on the flip side, he never took credit when we won.)

When my junior season ended, I had been happy for the team but unhappy with what I'd done as an individual. When my senior season concluded, I was unhappy with the final outcome when it came to our team but pleased with my personal contribution.

Back then, there were five recognized media outlets that selected the all-star teams. One of them was *Time* magazine, which was in its heyday among periodicals. Each week, an issue of *Time* arrived at our home, along with most of the homes I knew. One day, my phone rang. It was my parents. "Hey, go pick up a *Time* magazine for this week," they told me in an offhand manner. I wasn't sure what they were talking about, but when I opened it up, I saw a picture of myself and a write-up about my football career. I'd been selected as a first-team All-American. On top of that, I also made first-team All-Big Ten.

As a result, I was invited to play in the Lions American Bowl, the Senior Bowl, the Blue-Gray All-Star Game, and the Hula Bowl. I accepted the Blue-Gray invitation for no other reason than it was the first one I received. When the Hula

Bowl invitation arrived, I wished I'd held out. I could have gone to Honolulu for Christmas. Instead, I'd be spending it in Montgomery, Alabama, but as it turned out, the holiday had its perks.

The Blue-Gray Game was sponsored by the Montgomery Lions Club, with the money raised used to sponsor a local college student to study in Europe for a month. The young woman who'd been the prior year's recipient spoke at the players' dinner. Afterward, I ran into her in the parking lot, and we chatted. We ended up developing a bit of a friendship while I was in Montgomery, and she invited me to have dinner at her parents' house the night after the game. I happily accepted.

When I arrived, I discovered that her family lived in a rather exclusive area of town and had a butler and full waitstaff. Somewhat nervously, I took my place at the table, seated between my new friend and her father, who was at the head of the table. Across from us were her mother and younger sister. Once we were all seated, her father extended his hand toward me. I was used to this gesture from my own father, and so I did as was the custom in my house and handed him my plate so he could serve.

Wrong move!

In my family, we routinely said grace before dinner, but we never did it holding hands. Fortunately, we made it past my gaffe and had a nice evening. It was a lovely way to end the year.

As my senior season came to a close, I knew as little about what my future held as I had when I was a senior in high school and had no idea where I was going to go to college. The NFL draft was quickly approaching, but I was clueless about where I stood or what my chances were.

It seemed that someone had at least a hunch about what was in store for me. After our annual postseason banquet, our offensive line coach pulled me aside. "Hutch," he said, "good things are going to happen for you. If you ever need anything, come and see me." He didn't elaborate; he just walked away. I stood there, looking after him, puzzled. It was December, and the draft was two months away. Two whole months to sit with that cryptic statement.

Back then, the NFL draft was nothing like it is today. A team would turn in their selection, then call the player. If you got drafted, you'd get a phone call—simple as that.

The draft started at 9 a.m. sharp. That morning, my roommate, who also had draft potential, and I sat nervously in our room, staring at the phone. At about twelve minutes after nine, the phone rang. We looked at each other, startled. For the phone to ring so soon meant that someone had to have gone in the first round. That didn't sound right. We weren't just being modest—everyone pretty much knew who the first-round picks were likely to be, and we weren't among them.

As the second ring sounded, we continued to gape at one another in dead shock. Finally, our other roommate piped up. "I'll answer it!" he said and grabbed the receiver. "Hello?" Pause. "No, I'm sorry—you've got the wrong number," he said. I don't know who was on the other end of that call, but they had the worst timing ever.

Finally, hours later, the phone rang again. "Chuck Hutchison?"

"Yes, sir," I affirmed.

"You've been drafted by the St. Louis Cardinals in the second round."

Truth be told, I'd hoped to go to Cleveland or Cincinnati, but when it came down to it, I didn't really care who drafted me. I was delighted to be going to St. Louis. My roommate ended up getting a call, too, going in the sixth round to the Los Angeles Rams.

My selection in the draft meant I got to play in that year's

All-Star game, which took place at Soldier Field in Chicago. It was sponsored by the Chicago Tribune Charities, with all the money raised going to charity. As proud of myself as I was to be there, my ego didn't get the best of me. It didn't have a chance! The team comprised the first- and second-round college draft picks. We spent two and a half weeks practicing to play our opponent: the Kansas City Chiefs. They were the previous year's Super Bowl champions. I ended up starting, but whatever pride swelled in me quickly deflated, and all because of two children.

One day, I was coming off the practice field with another player, and two little kids came running up to us. "Can we get your autograph?" they asked excitedly, shoving papers and pens at us. We smiled and signed, then headed off to the locker room. As we were walking away, I heard one kid ask the other, "Who is that guy?" referring to me. The other boy looked at my signature.

"Oh, he's nobody," he said, then wadded up the paper and tossed it away. I laughed and shook my head. Maybe that's the price you pay for being an offensive lineman.

Unfortunately, based on the way I went on to play in that game, I had every expectation that I would remain a nobody. My performance affirmed the kid's words. I was beaten in pass protection so badly that I could not tackle the defensive lineman and prevent him from getting to the quarterback. I would later learn that such a move was called a "lookout block," because the lineman would turn to the quarterback and yell, "Look out!"

It was the culmination of my collegiate career. The transition from Ohio State to the pros was in some ways the same kind of blind leap I'd made from high school to college. But what I was about to discover was that the leap to the NFL was far greater. When you get to the pro level, less than 1 percent of college players have even been invited to camp, and only a small percentage of those guys actually make the team. Being drafted is absolutely no guarantee, and a collegiate career does not a pro career make.

I was now very well aware of the odds and of what was in front of me. It hit first during the All-Star game, and it hit even harder the next day, when I reported to Cardinals' training camp.

Part Two

CHAPTER 8

Going Pro

With only four hours of sleep the night before, I was in for a long two-hour drive from Soldier Field—where we'd played the All-Star game—to St. Louis's training camp. By 10 a.m., I was participating in my first practice as a professional. My head was spinning so fast I could not remember how to do jumping jacks during the warm-up. The morning practice lasted two hours, and the second practice in the afternoon was two and a half hours. Dinner was at six, followed by meetings from seven thirty until ten. This schedule prepared us for an exhibition schedule of six games.

The talent gap I experienced playing against the Chiefs in the All-Star game was not a mirage. With every day of training camp, I realized more and more that the difference in talent from college to pro was not a gap but a chasm. I was beginning to understand what the head coach meant when he told all of us rookies in our first meeting, "Gentlemen, you are here passing through to somewhere else." He did not mean leaving St. Louis and playing for another team; he meant being out of the

NFL as a career. Less than 50 percent of all players who made it their first year in the league played another two years. Three years in a profession does not a career make!

There were fifty rookies in camp, and we were all just a number with the same first name: Rookie. The coaches certainly wanted players to succeed, but they did not hold your hand. It was not like college, where the roster was set with the players you had to work with. In the pros, they could rotate players in and out like you change your socks. They didn't care who made the team and who did not. They were only interested in sourcing the best talent available.

During camp, there was this other rookie who kept screwing up. The offensive line coach walked right up to this kid and pointed to a plane that was flying overhead. "Son," he said, "do you see that jet?"

"Yes, sir."

"You keep screwing up, and you're gonna be on the next one." Plain as that.

The next day, the rookie continued to make mistakes, and predictably, the coach was on him again. "Son, do you love your momma?"

"Yes, sir."

"Well, you keep it up, and you're gonna see her tomorrow."

To an extent, the coach was kidding, but not by much. That was about how fast things happened.

It was an intense period of time. There were so many factors at play—injuries, personality conflicts, and so on—many of which were beyond your control. You were totally out of your comfort zone. All those factors combined to create an atmosphere where there's no point or place where you can look around, take a deep breath, and think, *I got this.* That kind of confidence was nonexistent for us new guys. Because what you thought you had, you didn't. And what you thought you didn't need, you did. And the faster you could find out which was which, the better off you'd be. I had four weeks of training camp and about six exhibition games to find those answers and show what I was capable of doing, and no one was going to help me.

There were four rookie offensive linemen, so it was hard for me to look at the rest of the line and gauge how I was doing. I knew I was getting my butt kicked, but I didn't know what the coaches' expectations were—I couldn't tell how I was performing in their eyes. I didn't know what their measurements were because I had no point of reference. It was like punching in the dark, and I didn't know which punches were landing and which ones weren't.

Off the field, things weren't any better. There was a tradition at St. Louis where the first- and second-round draft choices would have to stand up at dinner every night for a week and sing a song in front of the whole team. I believe I spent more time trying to learn songs than studying my playbook. I made a critical error one evening when I selected Peter, Paul and Mary's "Leaving on a Jet Plane," a tune that was popular at the time. As I sang, I realized its unfortunate relevance to my present circumstances. When I reached the chorus, the veterans began hooting and laughing, waving goodbye. "See ya!" they jeered. "Hope you're packed!"

For me, training camp was basically four to five weeks of "Oh shit!" moments back-to-back. I was constantly on edge, thinking about too many things that really weren't even related to football. My mind was filled with "What if this?" and "What if that?" Finally, I realized that if I didn't focus on the game and what I could manage, I was going to "What if" myself right out of the league.

As distracting as it all was, I did my level best to block out all those distractions, because you can get in your head and become paranoid pretty quickly. I knew that if I didn't get my mind right, it would be an easy decision for the coaches. So during those first few weeks, I sat down and had a talk with myself, which basically amounted to telling myself, *You'd better get going, or you're going to get gone.* Needless to say, it was a long summer.

You don't know whether you've made the team until the last cut-down, which takes place a week before the opening game of the season. Somehow, when the dust settled, I was still on the roster. I had survived. From a personal standpoint, I'd accomplished my primary objective. All told, of the fifty rookies who'd reported to camp, six of us made the squad, one on injured reserve. But as I'd quickly discover, that was just the first of many hurdles I'd have to clear.

Once you realize you're on the team, in the next few moments or hours, it dawns on you that you're going to need a place to live. I had to find a roommate and get set up in St. Louis, plus prepare for the season opener, all in that one week. There was no "Welcome to St. Louis!" No orientation or helpful tips—they just told you when to show up for practice the next day. And just because you'd made the team, that didn't mean you were going to stick around. In awareness of that fact, most of the veterans didn't even bother to learn my name; they just called me Rookie.

I spent the first year relegated to special teams, and I largely accepted my fate. I didn't expect to have a shot at starting—the veterans were just too much better than I was. Or at least, that's how I saw it.

I was putting in a ton of effort and, unlike in the past, seeing very little payoff. Still, by the end of the season, I had a better sense of where I stood, which made going into the second season a little bit easier. I had the lay of the land, and there were no surprises.

Still, in the three years I was with St. Louis, I never really settled in with the team, or in the town. I felt out of place in St.

Louis, and I didn't gel with the team's ownership. I felt like a puzzle piece that had been jammed into a space where I didn't quite fit.

Like anyone in their first job out of college, I was overwhelmed. I had more responsibilities than I'd ever had before, and I struggled to find my feet. In time, I learned to manage the details, but overall, being a pro athlete didn't hold the euphoria that I and everyone else thought it would.

On top of that, or perhaps in some way because of it, I began to sustain injuries. All through high school and college, I'd never so much as missed a practice, but now in the NFL, once the injuries started, they didn't let up. It was never anything major—a strained hamstring, a pulled groin, a dislocated elbow. Nothing required surgery, but all required that I miss a week or more of practice. It happened enough that I was labeled as injury-prone, and therefore unreliable.

I became disenchanted. After all, there was no way for me to make a difference on the team when I was sitting on the bench. There's a saying in the NFL: "You can't make the club in the tub." The rest of the team would be on the field practicing, and I'd be back in the training room getting treatment.

Still, I managed to make enough of an impact during my second season that as I entered my third, I was slated to start. Then, just before the opener, I hyperextended my knee. It felt like no matter how hard I tried, I just couldn't put anything together, and I couldn't build any momentum. And to be honest, I started to let it all get to me, and I'm sure it affected my play. Halfway through my second season, I had started asking the general manager to let me go. As time went on, my pleas became more insistent. Trade me, release me, anything. I didn't care; I just wanted out of St. Louis.

Going into my fourth year, just before the season started, I got my wish, yet it was at the worst time possible. I was released a week before the opening game of the season. At that

point, teams already had their rosters in place, so it was difficult, at best, to find a new home. I sat for about two months
with nowhere to go.

The Saints wanted to sign me, but I didn't want to go to
New Orleans. By that point, I knew that, to me at least, geography mattered. It had to be a good fit. Other teams expressed
interest, but none brought me in for a tryout.

One day, however, a call came in. It was from the Cleveland
Browns—the team that had been my favorite and that I'd
watched religiously all through my childhood. They wanted
me to come in for a tryout.

I flew to Cleveland and worked out for them, and the next
morning, they offered me a contract. I was signed to their
taxi squad, which was essentially a reserve group of players
who weren't on the regular roster but who could be activated
should the need arise. They called me up, and I saw action in
the last two games of the season. I was over the moon.

It wasn't just that I was playing for the Browns. When they
offered me the contract, they saw the terms I'd had with St.
Louis. The Cleveland owner told me I was so grossly under-
paid compared to the rest of the offensive line in Cleveland
that he simply had to do better by me. He gave me a significant
raise without me even asking for it. That was a class act. The
whole encounter refreshed me. It reignited my belief in myself
and built a foundation of trust in the team.

In St. Louis, it was like the sky had fallen on me. But by the
end of my fourth season in the pros, I was in the best position
I possibly could be, given my circumstances. As we moved into
the 1974 season, things were starting to look up.

One good thing did happen to me while I was in St. Louis.
I got married.

During the break after my rookie year in St. Louis, I returned
to Ohio State to take a few classes and work out on the old

campus. A guy I knew there was dating a girl, and the next thing I knew, she wanted to fix me up with a friend of hers, Ann. We ended up hitting it off, and what started as a blind date turned into an off-season romance.

As the new season rolled around, the Cards were slated to play an exhibition game in Cincinnati. Even though Ann and I had only known each other for seven or eight months, something just felt right. In retrospect, I can see that what I mistook for love was really just infatuation; yet at the time, I didn't know the difference. We decided to get married while I was in town for the exhibition game.

It was a Friday night game. I stayed over in Cincinnati, and we got married the next day. My schedule was locked up for the season, so our honeymoon amounted to the flight back to St. Louis. When we arrived, I carried Ann's bags into the apartment I'd rented for us, gave her a kiss, and headed off to practice.

Ann was twenty-one and I was twenty-three. We were really still just kids in many ways, with a lot to learn, not just about life and relationships but about each other. We hadn't been dating long enough to know much. We knew we enjoyed many of the same things, but that was the extent of it.

Looking back, I can see that it must have been hard being the wife of a rookie. I didn't have many relationships myself, so, socially, Ann was pretty much limited to the wives of the few friends on the team I did have. We also didn't have a lot of team functions, so there wasn't much opportunity for socializing. It wasn't a glamorous life. She liked going to the games, and she liked the notoriety, being the wife of a pro football player. At the same time, I was so unhappy with my performance on the team and my role that I probably wasn't always as enjoyable to be with as most new husbands are.

It did get a little easier the following year, as Ann started to make friends for herself and took on a few small modeling jobs, which perked her up. Plus, it was just the two of us, and we had few responsibilities, which meant that in the off-season, we could do what we wanted. We could travel or whatever we liked. It was fun, but it wasn't real life. It wasn't normal compared with what most people experienced. On top of that, we were in a kind of suspended animation because of my desire to seek a new team.

Whenever an issue arose in our relationship, my idea of resolving it was to stare at the ceiling until she'd stop complaining. When she told me that she was unhappy with something, I didn't have a sympathetic ear—I wanted it to blow over as fast as it could. It was probably more like my parents' relationship than I cared to admit.

My mother and father had little to no romance between them, at least that I saw. Their partnership was more utilitarian. It was about doing the things that life required, and they engaged in little conversation beyond what was necessary to accomplish that. They also showed little affection, except in the rare instance that there was something to celebrate.

I will say that Ann could not have been more different from my mother. Mom was fiercely independent and determined. She never complained, and she showed little emotion. She would have been a great middle linebacker. When she gave advice, it wasn't based on what might have been best for you mentally or emotionally but on her sense of morality—on what was the right thing to do.

Ann was the opposite. I remember one day, she said something that drove that point home to me about as much as anything she could have possibly uttered. She was lying on the couch, having taken a sedative because she didn't feel well. She said, "I don't believe that anyone should ever physically feel discomfort. No one should ever physically feel bad." I heard that and thought, *This is not going to end well.*

As time went on, it became apparent that we were deeply

and undeniably mismatched, and there seemed little hope of fixing things. Healthy relationships are built on trust and honesty. We did not trust each other enough to be honest, and so from there, our problems only intensified.

Fortunately, one thing had started to go well. Being back in Cleveland, combined with having a few years in the NFL under my belt, everything finally started to click. And since the move put us just a few hours away from Ann's parents, it improved both Ann's attitude and our marriage. I was in my home state, playing for a team I'd followed as a kid. Things felt familiar again, and as a result, my confidence increased. I was determined to make something out of the opportunity I'd been given.

Going into my fifth training camp, I was competing for a starting position, which I managed to secure. Finally, I started to feel like I belonged. Forrest Gregg, a man I greatly admired, was my line coach, then he was promoted to head coach. In my mind, everything was coming together.

Life blossomed in other ways as well. In 1974, my son Tyler was born, and I couldn't have been happier. Everything took on a new dimension, and the stakes for my success felt even higher. Suddenly, I had more responsibility, and I intended to live up to it.

Things were rolling along. I was making progress, accumulating experience, and doing the work, and I was finally seeing results. Our record the first half of the season was dismal, but it was Forrest's first year in the head-coach position, and sometimes those transitions take time to iron out. I had no doubt that Forrest had what it took to be a winning coach—it was simply a matter of effort over time. (And history would bear this out—that following year was indeed a winning season.)

It was the sixth game of the season, and we were playing the

Washington Redskins. The play we were running was a sweep. I had planted my right foot to turn upfield to lead the play when suddenly I heard a pop in my knee. I went down like I'd been shot. I hobbled off the field, and the docs gave me the once-over. Imaging revealed I had partially torn my anterior cartilage.

If I'd had the same injury today, it could have been fixed arthroscopically, and I'd have been home that evening in time for *Jeopardy* and back in the lineup in a few weeks. But at that time, cartilage surgery was a major procedure. The hope was that I could make it through the remainder of the season, then get surgery and rehab in the off-season.

This left me essentially unable to practice. If I took it easy enough during the week, I could play on Sunday. After the game, I had to have the knee aspirated, then let it settle down again for the next game.

Once the season ended, the team doctor performed the surgery, which left me in a cast for six weeks. I spent the entire off-season doing absolutely everything I could to rehab, but as the start of the new season approached, things still weren't feeling right. I'd gone through the entire training camp without being able to run without pain and swelling.

The training staff sent me to the Cleveland Clinic for another opinion. At that time, there was still an unspoken code among physicians that none would dare bad-mouth the work of another. Still, there was no mistaking the look on the doctor's face when he examined my knee. Clearly, the surgery had been botched. It would have to be redone. I spent the whole of 1976 on the injured list, awaiting my next procedure.

My orthopedic team at the clinic told me that my chances of walking again were very good, but my football career was very likely over. Still, I poured myself into my rehab and reported to training camp.

Sadly, the results were little better than after my first

surgery. I'd practice for a few days, then I wouldn't be able to walk, so I'd rest. It was wash, rinse, repeat.

With the final cut-down only a week away, I took a deep breath, walked into Forrest's office, and told him I was retiring. We both knew it was inevitable, but until the decision was made, I'd hung on to any glimmer of hope I could find. I was out of miracles.

My career in the NFL ended after seven seasons. I would miss being a part of a team, along with my teammates and a few good friends. I was grateful for the opportunity to experience life as a professional athlete, but in many ways, the game was entirely different from the one I'd played in high school and college. As an amateur, football is an experience, and decisions are made for the benefit of the team. Outcomes are celebrated or mourned together. Pro ball, however, is a business. Decisions and outcomes are financial. You can still develop that camaraderie with your teammates and the coaching staff, but in some ways, at the end of the day, it's an individual sport. In college, being a Buckeye was part of my identity. It was who I was. I experienced a sense of pride, honor, and belonging. Pro football was my job, and now it was time to find a new one.

After my last practice, I left Hiram College, where the training camp was being held, and drove home. I talked to a few reporters who'd gotten wind that I had retired.

The next day, when I woke up, I was no longer a professional football player. I had played forty-seven games in the NFL and started seventeen, but I had zero prospects of ever putting on pads or a helmet again. I was completely unmoored.

I did not know what I was going to do next, but I knew that whatever it was, I wasn't going to do it in Cleveland. I simply could not bear being so close to the team and the players I loved and *not* be a part of it. I didn't care what I did or where I did it, as long as it was somewhere else.

One of the hardest things for me to deal with was the lack of takeaways. Every time I'd struggled and failed in the past, as hard as it was, there was always something valuable I could learn from it. The Michigan loss was the biggest example. But as I lay there wondering what was going to become of my life, I couldn't think of a single insight or kernel of wisdom. It was as if a tornado had just blown through and demolished everything I'd worked for.

And maybe that was the lesson—that sometimes, you just get knocked so far off track that your life no longer resembles anything you recognize. The change is so sudden and so drastic that it leaves you completely disoriented, and the only thing you can do—the only choice you have—is to figure out how to get up. No grand plans, no pep talk, just working out the next step, no matter how small, that I needed to get on my feet.

Okay, I thought, *step one: Find a job.* I created a résumé, then I found a recruiter. Since I wasn't staying in Cleveland, my contacts there were no good, so I knew I'd need help.

As I looked ahead, the picture was completely black. I had no idea where my path was headed. All I knew was one thing: I had a wife, a child, and another on the way. It was my responsibility as a husband and a father to provide for them. Up to that point, I'd been playing games, literally. The life I'd lived bore little resemblance to the real world, and it was time to become an adult. I had to focus on putting my house in order. But as I was about to discover, there was more disorder there than I realized, and I was about to grow up very quickly indeed.

CHAPTER 9

Accidentally in Charge

Now that football was in the rearview mirror, it was time to find another way to earn a paycheck. I was no stranger to regular work. At the time, unless you had superstar status, being in the NFL wasn't enough to cover the bills. Like most players, I had jobs during the off-season. I did construction and sold steel, not because I particularly enjoyed the work or wanted to pursue it at some point in the future, but because it paid. Now, however, it was time to think long term.

I decided on a career in business. I had no experience. I didn't even know how businesses were structured—the various departments or how they functioned. But I needed to start somewhere, and the bottom was fine with me.

The headhunter I'd hired secured a few formal meetings where I met a handful of senior-level executives for lunch or a round of golf. It quickly became apparent that they were more interested in talking about pro ball or Ohio State than my future prospects. Something else became clear during those talks as well. Beyond football stories, any value I had to these people lay solely in my ability to make them money. If I couldn't bring anything to the table that could boost an organization's bottom line, I would remain unemployed.

After three long, agonizing months of searching, I was finally in the end-stage interview process for an entry-level marketing job. The position was with a rechargeable battery company whose North American headquarters was in Tampa, Florida. The ultimate decision would be made by the president of the company.

At the conclusion of the one-hour meeting, he asked me a question I dislike more than almost any other. He leaned back in his chair. "So," he said, "where do you want to be after five years with this company?" No matter how hard I ever thought about that question, I never came up with a good answer.

After a few long moments of thoughtful consideration, I said, simply, "In your chair."

He smiled and nodded, shook my hand, and thanked me for my time.

As the door closed, my stomach sank. I'd blown it! I'd intended for my reply to demonstrate my ambition, desire, and aggressiveness. Instead, he likely thought I was just a smart-ass.

I never did find out exactly what the president thought of my answer, but it must have been good, because somehow I got the job. I was officially an assistant marketing manager, and with that, we were on our way to Tampa.

In many ways, the move couldn't come soon enough. Not only was I anxious to start my job, but I also needed to get my family out of Ohio. It wasn't that there was anything inherently wrong with where we were, but we needed a change—a big one.

Running away from something without knowing where you are headed is generally a bad idea. Most of the time, you're just trading problems with few or no solutions. There are times when the decision is based solely on the lesser of two evils, and this was one of them. My decision to leave was influenced by my wife's well-being.

I had retired from the NFL in September, and our second son, Brady, was born four months later. He was five weeks premature. His lungs were not fully developed, and despite weighing in at a healthy six pounds, eleven ounces, and measuring twenty-one inches, he experienced seizures. He was placed in the ICU, where he remained for six days before we could take him home.

It was hard on both of us, but Ann's belief was that no one should be in pain, physical or emotional. Her coping mechanism was to take medication that had the effect of depressants. At the time, Brady needed constant care. He would experience tremors and brief periods of not breathing, and needed to sleep with his bed elevated to prevent fluid from forming in his lungs. Fortunately, I was home and could do whatever was needed. Ann's day was consumed with lying on the couch, watching television while smoking cigarettes. Hopefully, I thought, a change was what she needed, and our move would prompt her to once again become a responsible adult and mother.

Things started off fairly well in Florida, as I settled in for the three-month orientation. I anticipated that I'd continue along, learning my role and gradually moving forward. Yet suddenly the situation changed. After I concluded my onboarding, the company wanted me to relocate to one of their manufacturing plants. The dust from our move to Tampa had barely settled, and now we were headed off to Raleigh, North Carolina.

My task in Raleigh was to create an entry-level training manual for new hires. It was a big task, but not as big as the one I was about to step into. Four months into the work, the plant manager abruptly resigned, and I was selected to take his place. I was now the interim plant manager, leading 250 employees at a plant that was both unprofitable and plagued with safety issues. As I learned later, managers don't just up and leave good positions, and it would soon become apparent just why the previous manager had departed.

Of the company's five or six plants, ours was the worst-performing one.

The challenges were many, one of the biggest being employee turnover. It wasn't a great job, and it didn't offer great pay. Making batteries is inherently dangerous. When I took over, safety issues were a main concern. Sulfuric-acid burns and lead poisoning were not uncommon occurrences. In the local area, unemployment was roughly 3 percent. There were better options out there, so in many ways, we were an employer of last resort. Workers were largely demotivated, and in many cases, we simply had to take who we could get. Most of the employees didn't have an eighth-grade education, much less a high school diploma.

The managerial role was a demanding one in multiple respects. I was still relatively new to the company. Then, on top of the everyday demands of managing so many employees, plus the safety issues, we ran three shifts, so it wasn't uncommon for me to get calls in the middle of the night.

In 1973, Woody wrote a book titled *You Win with People*. As I contemplated the gargantuan task before me, I was reminded of something Woody used to talk about. In it, he repeated something I'd heard him say multiple times: "There is no such thing as great coaches, only great players." If you want to be an effective leader, you have to start with the belief that people are extremely important. It's something so many managers get wrong—they overfocus on results instead of the human beings behind them. Over my career, I've seen that to be consistently true, and it's the differentiation in success between companies that otherwise have all the same processes. The difference between winning and losing is how people are being led. I would rather have a team of less talented players who perform to the maximum level of their capabilities than a more talented squad who underperforms.

In sports, Woody invested in learning how each of us was motivated. He knew what was important to each of us. He learned our inner workings. Those weren't things we told him—he observed them. When it was my turn to step into a leadership role, I recognized that I couldn't motivate anyone until I understood something about who they were. Everyone had something that incentivized them or flipped their trigger. The most successful leaders are those who find the trigger for as many people as possible.

With some notion of that in mind, I called a meeting with my plant supervisors. "I have a question for you," I said. "How many of you can give me the names of five people who report to you?" Of the seven managers assembled before me, only one responded in the affirmative. *Okay*, I thought, *that's where we'll start.*

I shared with them a story about Woody. After home games, families would often assemble outside the stadium to wait for their sons, and inevitably, Woody would go out and strike up conversations with them. As the season went on, he learned the names of everyone—mothers, fathers, siblings—along with some information about each of them. "Gentlemen," I said to my new reports, "you cannot lead people you do not know, and people will not follow leaders who don't know them."

Then, for good measure, I told them another Woody story, this one involving my sister. She had elected to attend OSU as well, and the day she arrived as a freshman, Woody personally went to her dorm room to greet her. Not only that—he gave her his home phone number and told her to call should she ever need anything.

"We're going to improve this business, but not through anything we do," I told the managers. "We can't change processes, and we can't change employees. What we have is what we've got. It may be ugly, but it's our ugly, so it's up to us to improve it. What we need to improve is our employees, but we don't just need them to perform better; we need them to communicate more. They're the ones who are out there on the line, and so they are the ones who are best positioned to see what's going wrong and how best to fix it. But if they don't raise their hand and tell us, there's nothing we can do. So it's got to start with them. And as far as I'm concerned, every failure and every mistake that's made going forward is a failure of leadership."

The problem was that communication at the plant only went one way—from the managers to the employees. As a result, the workers just did their jobs, hoped they didn't get grief from management (or get injured), and went home. We had to find a way to get them more engaged. To care. And that meant showing we cared about them.

I called three all-staff meetings, one with each shift. First, I shared with them some insights on where we stood performance-wise. Then, I outlined our objectives and how we planned to meet them. "But the only way we're going to reach these goals is because of you—every person in this room," I said. "You are the people who make it all happen, or not. I want you to know that it's on us as the managers to help you. Now, I don't know much about all of you—not really. I don't know what makes you happy or what makes you sad, or what your goals are. All that takes more time to learn than we have right now. But I want you to know that I have an interest in one thing, and that's how I can help you. Not just on the line and in your work, but as an individual. I will only be as good at that as what you're willing to share." I told them they weren't required to give me all the details of their life or to share anything personal if they didn't want to, but if there was something that I or their manager could do that would help them, our doors were open.

I doubt they'd ever heard such talk from a boss before, and that was my primary goal—to disarm them. I wanted to shake things up for them perceptually so that they'd be open to a new way of doing things. So they'd understand we were taking a new approach, and that approach involved putting them first. But this was also a new approach for the managers, so I had to figure out how to help them be successful as well.

Dale Carnegie once said that a person's name is to them "the sweetest and most important sound in any language." I began to hold meetings with the managers three times per week. I told them we'd start with the fundamentals, which is always a good place to start. I gave them simple, specific assignments, starting with names. Learn the names of everyone who works for you. Ideally full names, but at least start with first names. Once they had that down, we built on it. I started asking them to learn things about the employees' families and their children, or other things about their lives outside the plant.

When it came to the actual work, we devised ways to set employees up for success. We gave them attainable goals, and we recognized when they achieved them. We found as many positive things as we could to acknowledge, no matter how small they seemed. We gave out little badges for people who came to work seven days in a row. Those things cost very little, aside from some attention and effort on our part as managers, and they may seem like nothing, but they were effective, because our excitement and appreciation were genuine.

Our success in getting the employees to trust us was crucial. They had to understand that anything we asked them to do differently was in some way going to benefit them. People see through phony stuff in a heartbeat. We were sincere, we were consistent, and we followed through. We began to handle accidents differently, not simply blaming the workers, as had happened in the past, but instead trying to find out what had gone wrong and what we could change so it was unlikely to happen again. Because we were honest and straightforward with them and because we walked our talk, the employees were willing to give us a chance.

After a few months, there was a noticeable shift in the environment. Instead of going drudgingly about their work, then sitting and staring on their breaks, employees were having conversations with one another and even with managers. Once in a while, they even looked like they were enjoying what they were doing.

Finally, after I'd served ten months as interim plant manager, a permanent manager was hired. The operation he took over was scarcely recognizable from the one I had inherited. During my tenure, every plant measurement improved, from employee retention to production and profitability metrics to safety.

As I now realize, this marked the first time in my life I actually utilized the leadership philosophy I would come to rely on: believing that true leadership is about your ability to make other people successful. In that way, it was really just like coaching, and most of the same ideas and skills applied.

While I was proud of our accomplishment, I was happy to move on. Being a plant manager wasn't something I envisioned doing any longer than I had to. Fortunately for me, life had a similar notion.

One afternoon, as I was finishing my transition out of my interim role, the phone rang.

"Hey, Hutch," the voice on the other end said, "do you still have the itch?"

The caller was Forrest Gregg, my old coach in Cleveland. He'd just left Cleveland and been named head coach of the Canadian Football League's Toronto Argonauts.

"How'd you like to be my offensive line coach?" he asked.

I considered his question for a fraction of a second.

"When do I start?"

Life is not linear. You rarely go from one endeavor to the next in a logical, rational pattern. It's often more like a zigzag. But what's more important than the path is the trend. Are you trending toward personal growth, experience, exposure, and challenges? If you are, you're on your way to achieving your best.

CHAPTER 10

Scratching the Itch

Two weeks after Forrest's call, we were on our way to Toronto. It was hard to believe that within two years of retiring from the NFL, at the age of thirty-two, I found myself back in professional football. Of course I'd considered a career in coaching, but nothing seemed realistic. Coaching high school would require that I go back to college and get a degree in education. I didn't want to coach at the college level, because I didn't want to deal with the recruiting process. And without prior experience in college ball, there was no way I'd get a coaching position in the NFL. I wasn't averse to working my way up, but as someone who had a family to provide for, I didn't see a lot of prospects in being an assistant to an assistant. Forrest's offer came at just the right time, from just the right person.

As with so many opportunities that arise in life, this one resulted from a personal connection. One of the best ways to predict whether someone is going to be successful is if you've worked with them in some capacity before. Even if there isn't a direct connection, we often seek out referrals. That's because, whether it's hiring an accountant for your business or a handyman for your house, we tend to turn to our own network first. When you're doing your job and you're doing the absolute best you can, putting in that work, people notice, and they're likely to remember.

Forrest knew me, and he knew the requirements to be a successful coach. You needed to be passionate, detail-oriented, a good communicator, a good motivator, both trustworthy and willing to trust others, and of course knowledgeable in the fundamentals and techniques of play—and you had to be able to evaluate people's talent and get a sense of what they were capable of.

I didn't realize it then, but all that time I spent injured with the Browns had an upside. During the periods when I was unable to play, I would help the team by scouting our opponents, analyzing the players and their tendencies, and sharing that info with the coaching staff. Forrest knew me as more than a player—he'd seen me develop broader skills as well. Because of that, he was confident I could handle the role as assistant coach, and I was thrilled for the opportunity.

We rented a home in Oakville, Ontario, about twenty miles from the stadium. It was the same field where the Toronto Blue Jays baseball team played.

Yet even though the Argonauts were a professional team, this was not the NFL. Canadian football wasn't quite at the level of football in the States. That's not to disparage the players or the league; it's just that while football gets top billing in the US, in Canadian athletics, the marquee sport is hockey. My entire offensive line consisted of Canadians who had played college ball in their home country. Most of them had aspired to play professional hockey, but as they grew older, it became apparent that they didn't have the skills to excel in such a competitive league. Professional football was their alternative. My players had roughly the same level of talent as a Division II college team in the US. But I wasn't concerned about having a line full of guys for whom football was their plan B. After all, it had been mine, too, until I gave up baseball in my early years.

While my squad may not have been the most talented as individuals, the whole was greater than the sum of its parts. As a unit, they consistently played at a high level. I found them all to be motivated, hardworking, and very coachable. There was a lot they didn't know, but they were eager to learn. We focused on fundamentals and basics—things like footwork and head position. Given their limited skills, I really had to coach, which was great for me in terms of developing my own skills. The players were working hard and I was, too. Using many of the same drills and techniques I'd learned from my line coach at Ohio State, in good time, I was able to bring my line to a competitive level.

Finally, it seemed like I was once again hitting my stride, at least professionally. I enjoyed what I was doing. It was both challenging and rewarding, and the team had started to feel like I was where I belonged.

That was, until the phone rang.

Our move from Cleveland to Tampa hadn't done anything to resolve Ann's substance-abuse problem, which followed us to Florida, then to North Carolina. Perhaps the string of upheavals actually contributed to it. I'll never know.

Over the years, as so many addicts and their families experience, Ann was in and out of treatment programs, from therapy and clinics to short stints in rehab facilities. But each time, in short order, she'd be back using again. Perhaps our continued relocations actually helped her get the drugs. Her pattern was to obtain illegal prescriptions through doctors' practices, lying about who she was and her symptoms. In each town, she was able to get all the drugs she needed from irresponsible physicians by falsifying her identity.

During my first off-season with the Argonauts, I got a call from the Royal Canadian Mounted Police. Ann had been arrested obtaining drugs illegally. The RCMP was not about second chances, and they issued an ultimatum—Ann had forty-eight hours to leave the country, never to return, or report to prison. The next day, her parents drove up from Ohio, picked up their daughter, and brought her back to live with them in the States. Just like that, I had two young children, ages four and six, to care for on my own.

Very quickly, I developed an appreciation for single parents, as well as community. When friends and neighbors heard what had happened, they swung into action. Fortunately, because it was the off-season and I was working essentially nine to five, there were fewer demands on my time, and my schedule wasn't so erratic. Then, the start of football season roughly coincided with the start of the school year. Tyler entered second grade, and Brady started kindergarten. My dear, wonderful neighbors who lived just a few blocks away pitched in by watching the boys after school every evening until I returned home. On weekends, I took the boys to practice with me, and they had a great time hanging out with the players and staff. When I had to travel, they'd spend the night with the neighbors until I got home the next day and picked them up.

My grandfather, Art, used to say, "You don't need a lot of friends, just a few true ones." These neighbors and the others who helped out were exactly that. They basically adopted us, and I will forever be grateful for their kindness. I truly could not have managed during that time without the goodwill and generosity of these incredible people.

For much of my life, I'd focused on developing myself—on doing the mental and physical work that would help me improve and give me a shot at being successful in life. It was at this time that I first realized just how important the externals are. The fact is no one ever becomes truly successful alone. It's essential to develop ourselves, but we also want to reach beyond our own boundaries and cultivate community. Because whether it's the potential employers who call us up when there's an opening, or the friends and neighbors who help us out when we're in need, life is a team sport.

For even the most self-sufficient person, there will be times when you'll need to cry uncle. For me, those times are relatively easy to recognize. I know I've gotten there when I've exhausted all available possibilities, or I've arrived at the boundaries of my knowledge or capabilities, yet I still haven't resolved the most critical need. In that case, the first step I take is to consider who I can reach out to who would be best positioned to satisfy that need.

Many times, when we're faced with a crisis, we use a shotgun approach, firing off a broad burst of pellets, but that can create more problems than it solves. In my experience, it's far more beneficial to take a more thoughtful, targeted approach.

Once, my town was hit by a major storm. We made out okay, but one of our friends had a tree that went right through their house. Understandably, they panicked. Immediately, they sent out messages to every group they were a part of, including posting on Facebook, asking for help. They were met with a deluge in response. There was a ton of input, and the problem was that most of it was noise. I could tell it was difficult to sort through all the responses and figure out the best way to proceed—what action would provide the most immediate and effective solution.

Instead, you want to drill down on exactly what you need— to identify the top priority first. Then, you go in that direction. Do you need someone to come and remove the tree, or do you need to get the roof covered? Maybe the damage is extensive enough that you can't stay in the house, and what you really need to do first is find a temporary shelter. Then, you can figure out what needs to be done about the house. When you're focused at this level, you know who to talk to and what questions to ask, and they understand what you need and how to help. Everyone knows the priority and is focused on the mission. In my experience, that's how you find the best solution in the shortest amount of time possible.

I came by that awareness through football. That's essentially what you're doing in the course of a game. When someone is injured, you have to figure out who will replace them. You also have to decide how it's going to affect your game plan. Do you stick to your original strategy or change it up? All these decisions are made one step at a time.

Granted, this might not be in your character. Being good in a crisis simply isn't a strength for everyone. I know it's not for my wife. And she knows it, too, so she has a backup plan— me. When something big happens and we need to act quickly, she knows I will be the one to come up with the plan. She can help with the execution. So you either need to be someone who can ignore the noise and not get overwhelmed or paralyzed by all the potential distractions, or you need to have someone you can turn to who can. It all comes back to knowing your own strengths and weaknesses. You might be able to develop this muscle, but perhaps not, and that's okay. You just need to have that capability somewhere in your network.

During that period after Ann left, the most important thing to me was to give the boys as normal a life as I possibly could. I tried to be both dad and mom. Tyler and Brady pitched in, making their beds and cleaning up their dishes after breakfast. The laundry was a group effort. We developed routines we'd follow every day like clockwork, unless, of course, one of the boys got sick, which threw us into survival mode. But we figured it out.

When it came to cooking, I did my best. I called my mother and asked for recipes for dishes I remembered her making when I was a kid. One of the highlights of the month became the PTA meetings, where I got to exchange recipes with the moms.

It was a lot to handle, but we made it work. That went on for about six months, until we took another blind hit—one that would rock me harder than anything I'd ever experienced.

I was scheduled to travel to the States for a scouting trip to look at some college players. The boys were on spring break, and because they hadn't seen their mother since she'd left Canada, I thought it would be a good opportunity for them to spend some time with her. When we arrived in Ohio, I dropped off the kids at Ann's parents' house, then went about my trip. When I returned to pick them up for our flight back to Toronto, Ann had news for me.

"Where are the boys?" I asked.

"They're not here," she said, then told me she'd gone to court. She reached out and handed me some documents. They were custody papers. She said the boys would be staying with her.

I was flabbergasted. Shocked and desperate, I appealed to Ann's parents, but to no avail. "Children deserve to be with their mother," they said.

For two days, I searched, trying desperately to find my sons. I spoke with my attorney, who'd been investigating my options.

"Chuck," he said, "I'm afraid you have to give it up. At least for now." I refused to accept what he was saying, but he explained that if I did find the boys and took them back to Toronto, I could be charged with kidnapping.

It took a few minutes for it all to sink in. For the moment, at least, I had no choice. The courts didn't care at all that Ann had been kicked out of the country we'd been living in or had a history of drug abuse. They didn't care about a father who'd done everything he possibly could to provide the love and stability his children needed. All they saw was a mother who wanted her kids back.

I flew back to Toronto alone, devastated, and betrayed. I wasn't just low, I was underground, looking up from the absolute bottom.

The court calculated the child support that was due to Ann, and the exchange from Canadian to US dollars did not favor me. Once the money was deducted from my paycheck, I was left with somewhere between fifty and a hundred dollars per month—not nearly enough to live on. I vacated the home we'd rented and, with nowhere else to go, moved my few personal belongings into the Argonauts' facility, beneath the stadium. The area consisted of meeting rooms, coaches' offices, the players' locker room, and a training room. For five months, a training table served as my bed.

I will say that this arrangement did offer a few perks. For one, I was never late for a meeting. On top of that, during baseball games, I had access to all the popcorn and hot dogs I cared to eat. It was a meager existence, but at least I wasn't going into debt. Once again, I was making it work.

That time in my life, and for many years going forward, was filled with challenges. Some of them were logistical; many were emotional. When I look back on it now, it was nothing short of insane.

What got me through was something I've had my whole life, which is an ability to compartmentalize. No matter what was happening, it was like the more stressful it got, the more I was able to tune in and focus on the present. The more chaotic things were, the more I could zero in on what needed to be done in that moment. To stay grounded.

To some extent, I think people either have this ability or

they don't, but if it's there in some capacity, it can be developed. For me, I think it was honed in part by farming, and from there on, it grew into a strength.

To others, it didn't always seem like a strength. Sometimes, in dire circumstances, what people need is to connect emotionally, but in that mode, I simply couldn't. I couldn't go there, otherwise I wouldn't have been able to do what I needed to do because I would have been too bogged down in my feelings. Plus, I didn't know any other approach. It's what came naturally to me, to tune in, pay attention, and focus on the details. If something didn't work, just let it go and keep moving.

Of course, I thought about my boys constantly. I missed them like crazy. But I couldn't allow myself to dwell on that, because at least for now, there was nothing I could do to change the situation. So for the time being, I went into my default mode—I put my head down and just did the work, one day after another.

Shortly into my tenure with the Argonauts, Forrest was tapped to become the head coach of the Cincinnati Bengals. Our defensive back coach, Willie Wood, was elevated to the top spot in Toronto. As I'd seen and was about to experience firsthand, coaching can be like a traveling road show in terms of how many times you move on.

Coaches know that their fortunes can shift with the wind. Lou Holtz used to joke about being let go from Notre Dame. At the time, the athletic director commented that Holtz was fired because he was "tired and burned out." Holtz framed it slightly differently. As he frequently quipped when speaking at banquets, "I was fired because of illness and fatigue. The fans were sick and tired of me."

When my third season in Toronto came to a close, the entire coaching staff got our walking papers. That's when I learned that there are two types of coaches—those who have been fired and those who are going to get fired.

It would be another six months before the NFL season ended and coaching positions would open up, so in the meantime, I needed to find work. With no more ties to Toronto, I decided to move back to Cleveland. I rented a room in my old neighborhood from some close friends who lived three houses down when I played for the Browns.

I borrowed tools and took on odd jobs, building patios, walkways, and retaining walls for people I knew in the neighborhood. The boys were living in Dayton, a few hours away. I was able to see them a few times for supervised visits, but in some ways, that almost felt worse than not seeing them at all. Under the specter of observation and knowing that our time was limited, we couldn't just be ourselves or simply enjoy one another. Still, it was the best I could manage at the time, and at least they knew I was still there for them in any way I could be. I hadn't given up on them.

Five months into my time back in Cleveland, the phone rang once again.

This time, it was John Ralston, who'd been a head coach for both Stanford University and the Denver Broncos. We'd become friends when he visited the Argonauts' training camp. At that time, there was a new football league forming—the United States Football League (USFL). It was intended that the twelve teams would play during the spring in the NFL's off-season. The goal was to offer football fans more of what they loved and, in so doing, capture their sports dollars.

John said he'd taken a position as head coach for the new Oakland Invaders. They were scheduled to play their first game in six months—in March 1983 at the Oakland Coliseum—but he needed an offensive line coach. He felt I was the right guy for the job, but the final approval needed to come from the owner, so off I flew to San Francisco.

It was a memorable meeting. After several hours of chatter, mostly by the owner, he informed me that he was not only offering me the job but also expanding my role. In short, my other duties would boil down to essentially everything that was needed to field the team in time for our first game. Among other jobs, I would have to scout and sign more than one hundred players, secure a practice facility and a training campsite, hire a support staff, and of course perform the duties of offensive line coach. In essence, I would be the general manager. My total budget for payroll was a million dollars, the equivalent of an NFL third-round signing bonus.

For the owner's part, he would take on two critical tasks: choosing the team's colors and selecting the cheerleaders.

With an offer like that, how could I say no?

Knowing I had no better prospect of seeing my boys if I was in Cleveland versus Oakland, off I went to the West Coast.

CHAPTER 11

Hallelujah!

One challenge I did not have when I landed in Oakland was housing. The owner of the Invaders also owned a condo complex. One unit was converted to the team's office, and I took up residence in the unit directly above. The setup was perfect, as it enabled me to immerse myself in the many tasks required to get the team up and running. That was helpful from a productivity standpoint, but it was also good for me mentally and emotionally. The gargantuan undertaking provided a useful distraction from the anguish of missing my boys.

My day started at 5 a.m. sharp, when I would get on the phone with the East Coast, soliciting feedback from past coaches on players I was interested in signing. I would then work my way across the time zones until finally hanging up the phone around 8 p.m. Then I would work out, eat some dinner, and head to bed. The next day, it started all over again.

In addition to scouting, we held open tryouts. It seemed like every Walter Mitty who ever wanted to play professional football appeared. We had more than four hundred guys show up over three separate tryouts. A cab driver who'd shuttled multiple hopefuls to the field finally asked one of them what was going on. When he learned about the open call, he hopped out of his cab, kicked off his shoes, and joined in.

While the numbers were massive, it was relatively easy to pare the groups down. After running the forty-yard dash and some other basic drills, each squad whittled down to roughly thirty or forty potentials. Out of those tryouts, we signed about ten guys. Three of them went on to make the team, and two ended up as starters. The remainder of the team consisted of players who'd been released from the NFL or played semi-pro ball, or who were taken during the USFL draft.

On March 6, 1983, the Oakland Invaders played their in-augural game before a crowd of over forty-five thousand fans. Our team of forty-five players and twenty-five cheerleaders, all decked out in blue and gold, were ready for action. The owner and I had each made good on our responsibilities.

We won that first game and went on to finish the season 9–9, securing the Pacific Division title. Unfortunately, we did not carry our success into the second season, which opened with a bumpy start, as we lost our first three games. The night of that third loss, I was summoned to the owner's house. There, he told me he'd fired John Ralston, the head coach. He had a press conference scheduled for the following day, at which he planned to announce that he'd appointed me as the interim head coach. Then, he looked at me expectantly.

I told him I was grateful for the vote of confidence and I indeed hoped to one day become a head coach, but that day was not today. I did not wish to lead the team with its current construction. I knew we had the talent to win, but we lacked discipline and an effective offensive strategy. We also didn't have the coaching talent on staff. So, respectfully, I declined.

He sized me up for a moment. "Let me make this clear," he

said. "If you wish to remain employed by the Invaders, it will be as the interim head coach."

"What time is the press conference?" I replied.

In sports, you never know when your number is going to be called. That's why I always thought it was way more difficult to be a backup player than a starter. As a backup, all the performance expectations are there, but you don't get the same preparation. Instead, you spend a lot of time in the unknown, trying to stay ready. We can find ourselves in a similar place in other walks of life as well. You never know when things will shift, and suddenly you'll be in a position where you're expected to make something happen, so ideally you do your best to stay primed. You prepare as if you're going to start, then learn to hang out on standby.

I had that same expectation about leadership—that someday my number would be called. I had been in and around some incredible football programs, and I knew what it took to be a head coach. At Ohio State, I spent four years surrounded by some high-quality people. They were top-notch human beings who also knew their trade exceptionally well. My greatest takeaway from that time wasn't a national championship but my preparation for life. We all left that program knowing we could handle whatever life had in store for us. I didn't know when or how I'd get to apply the information I'd garnered—whether in football or elsewhere—but I was aware that it was invaluable. In the end, nearly all my peers at Ohio State ended up in leadership or other influential roles, and that was because we knew two things: We knew how to elevate ourselves, and we knew how to deliver outstanding results. Once that's in you, it's in you, and you're prepared to apply it.

As an assistant coach, I added to that knowledge base, gathering information I thought I'd need as a head coach. So even though the position was thrown into my lap overnight, I had some reasonable expectation that I could handle it. At the time, I was one of the youngest head coaches in football. All the others in the USFL had been head coaches either in the NFL or at the college level. Yet I was the best person suited for the role at the time, and I knew it.

I accepted the position under the condition that I'd be empowered to choose the players and coaches and could make all the decisions affecting football operations. My plan was simple: Put the players and coaches in the best position to be successful. Work on the fundamentals, and build from there. I told the owner that this would likely lead to more losses in the short term, but it would enable the kind of continual improvement that would eventually render us competitive. For myself, I reasoned that if I couldn't turn things around, then at least I knew it would be of my own doing rather than a result of having to acquiesce to someone else's terms.

While I was able to convince the owner to let me do things my way, a tougher task remained. As the person who'd been responsible for negotiating the players' contracts, I'd had to tell the players that they placed a higher value on themselves than I did. In other words, I didn't think they were worth the money they wanted to be paid. The fact was I didn't have a lot to work with financially, so I had to hold a hard line. Now, I had to turn around and convince these same guys that I believed in them. I could imagine them thinking, *Who does this guy think he is?* only in more colorful language. In that way, it was like the battery company all over again, so I started at the same place—building trust.

At least I had street credit in football. But that was only going to last as long as I made good on that credit and actually showed the players I could make them and the team successful.

The most enduring trust is built over time, and the easiest way to undermine your efforts is to be inconsistent. I needed to be up-front with the team about what they could expect from me, then follow through each and every minute. Without that, we didn't have a prayer.

When I stepped in front of the group, the first thing I did was acknowledge their doubt and, in some cases, their flat-out animosity toward me. I explained that what I had to do to be successful in my previous role was my job, not my belief. It was nothing personal. The thing that mattered was what I believed about each of them as individuals and about the Invaders as a team.

"Here's the plain truth," I said. "Some of you who are starters today will be moved to different positions. I know some of you will be happy with these changes, while others will be anything but. Yet here's the thing: If we maintain the status quo simply so that everyone is happier and there will be less turmoil in the short term, well, we already know what that will produce in the long term. We've already lost our first three games, and I guarantee we'll lose our next fourteen. I'm not interested in going 0 and 18 and having my name attached to that, and I believe the same is true of you."

I put myself in their minds and figured that we all wanted the same thing, which was to win. I wasn't naive enough to think that this, on its own, would do the trick—that it would be a one-and-done conversation—but this was the start. From then on, I tried to reinforce the same message every day—that my only motivation was to do things that would help us win. And I took advantage of every single opportunity to reinforce it on an individual level as well. The credibility I brought with me from my experience in football made the players and coaches pay attention to me. Once you have that attention, trust is built from what they hear and see.

I knew that trust would be the keystone of our success, because without it, there's nothing to build on. If you don't have undivided trust, you have nothing. There's no way forward.

Typically, when there's a breakdown in relationships, businesses, or families, it is in some way due to a lack of trust. When we see everything as "us" and "them," there's no hope for a "we."

Unlike in other settings, on sports teams you have total visibility. As the head coach, you're surrounded by your squad, constantly interacting with them. You're not like a CEO who can go off to their office and close the door. In sports, there's nowhere to hide. Everyone has a high level of exposure. You share in the same challenges, and you share in the same results, so there's a strong responsibility to one another to perform.

During this time, I often thought back to the head coach I had in my second year in St. Louis. He was hired from the Minnesota Vikings, where he had been the defensive coordinator. The Vikings' head coach for whom he'd worked had a reputation for never changing his demeanor. Regardless of the circumstance, he was always stone faced, calm, and stoic. Throughout training camp, our new head coach emulated his former boss. That is, until the last game of the exhibition season. A player made a costly mistake, and when he reached the sidelines, instead of reacting in a manner we had come to expect, the coach went berserk. His arms were flailing; he was cursing at the top of his lungs and throwing things. He lost it. From that day forward, he also lost the team. No one felt they knew him or trusted him. He never regained the relationship with the players that he needed for the team to win. He was fired after his second year.

Especially when you're in a leadership position, people need to know who they're going to see day in and day out. It's true of coaches, it's true of managers and executive leadership, and it's true of teachers and parents. When my oldest son, Tyler, was four or five years old, he loved to do this thing where he'd just walk up to the TV and turn it off while we were watching it. This was before remote controls. I'd tell him, "Tyler, don't do that." And when he did it again, I'd tell him again. If I didn't tell him that the tenth time he did it, I might as well not have told him times one through nine. You need to be consistent. It's not about whether you tend to be fiery or keep your cool; it's that others know what to expect of you.

If you want people to trust you, you have to be worthy of their trust. You have to be open and honest. You have to speak from the heart. People need to know that you're like them—that you hurt like them and laugh like them. You're a real person. And again, they need to know you're dedicated to making them successful, however they define that. If they feel like you are truly engaged in their success and well-being, they will follow you anywhere and do anything for you.

As I reorganized my players and coaches, I revisited one of Woody's core philosophies—that a coach's responsibility is to identify what people can do and put them in the best position to do it. To give them the resources to be successful, then get out of their way.

To that end, I dismissed two assistant coaches and the offensive coordinator and replaced them with coaches who'd been recommended by people I trusted. Several players switched positions or were replaced by reserve players who I believed had better potential if only they saw more playing time. I did this all in my first week. From there, I focused not on who we were playing each week, but on what we needed to do to become stronger. What our opponents were doing was of no importance, only what we were doing.

My first game as head coach was against the Philadelphia Stars, in Philadelphia. They'd won the league championship the year before and were looking even better that season.

The morning of the game, as I looked out my hotel window, I glanced at the street sign below. It read "Hutchison Street." Figuring it was surely an omen, my optimism soared.

At halftime, we were up 7–0, and I was even more certain

of a victory. Yet in the second half, unfortunately for us, the Stars began to play up to their ability, and we lost 28–7. We also went on to lose our next five games, closing out the first half of the season 0–9. But as I'd predicted to the owner, even though we had yet to win, the team was improving. Each week, they were getting better, and it was because they continued to do everything I asked of them.

I told the players that our situation was very much like that of a golfer who has a disappointing front nine and decides to reset their thinking, casting the back nine as an entirely new round. Poised to start the next nine games, we entered the start of our *second* second season.

Game ten was an out-of-town matchup against the Chicago Blitz. Joining the team for the first time in game play was a defensive back I'd moved to running back during my first week as head coach. He'd played defensive back at Purdue but had been a running back in high school. I switched him to offense because he had great speed, and he was the only guy we had with the ability to make big plays.

For the previous four weeks, the running back had been on the reserve squad, learning the position. This week would be his coming-out party, and he did not disappoint. On the very first play of the game, he took the handoff and ran seventy-five yards for a touchdown. With that explosive play setting the tone, we went on to win our first game of the season.

Entering the locker room afterward, I expected to come upon a major celebration. I was surprised, then, at the fairly subdued tone. Typically, when a team wins, especially after a long dry spell, the atmosphere is all high fives and jubilation. There's a release of pent-up frustration. But I observed none of that.

Then it hit me. This season's team had only ever experienced losing. They were conditioned to it, and their reaction was similarly conditioned. Many times, I had experienced the electricity and exaltation that comes with winning. Being in the locker room after Ohio State won the Rose Bowl was very nearly an out-of-body experience. The Invaders deserved to experience that feeling, and I was going to make sure they did.

I grabbed a stool and called the team together. Then I stood atop the stool, so I'd be positioned over everyone.

"Hey, guys," I said. "How many of you have ever heard a Baptist minister say the word 'hallelujah'?" As I anticipated, many raised their hands. "Well, when they say 'Hallelujah!' or 'Praise the Lord!' how do they say it? What's the tone? Is it ordinary or subdued? Of course not. They bellow. Their voice is full of joy, triumph, and praise! Well, your victory has all of that, and it deserves the same response. Now come on and give me a 'Hallelujah'!"

It took several attempts, but they finally reached a pitch worthy of a preacher. It was a glorious moment, and one of my favorite memories of my entire life.

The opening play of our next game was like watching a play-back of the previous week. Our new secret weapon ran the ball eighty-three yards on the opening play. Once again, we came out victorious, and this time, the locker room atmosphere was as it should be following a win. I stood on the stool and led the team in two riotous hallelujahs.

Believe it or not, the third game started exactly the same way as the first two, with our star running back scoring from scrimmage on the very first play. To my knowledge, he became the first player in professional football history to score on the first play from scrimmage in three consecutive games. It was also the team's third straight victory. We enjoyed three well-deserved hallelujahs!

The day after our third win, I was scheduled to introduce Coach Hayes at a large Ohio State alumni banquet in San Francisco. I'd given a fair number of speeches before that, but introducing my idol was nerve-racking. Still, I got through it, then returned to my seat at the head table.

Coach Hayes was about ten minutes into his remarks when he stopped abruptly and turned toward me, glaring. "What are you still doing here?" he blasted in front of the entire audience. "You're not going to beat anyone by sitting here listening to me. Get back to the work." With that, I slid out of my seat and walked off stage. It was the longest walk I'd taken since the time he'd sent me to the locker room at the start of my senior year. But win on Sunday, we did. Hallelujah number four!

With three more victories, our record for the second half of our second season stood at 7–0. After bellowing out seven hallelujahs, the team was nearly hoarse, but they were eager for number eight. I think they were more interested in protecting their string of hallelujahs than consecutive wins.

Our late-season comeback positioned us to play for the division championships. We would take on our rivals for the championship, the LA Express. The Express had significant backing, including a payroll that was four times larger than ours. They were a strong team with several players who'd go on to have solid careers in the NFL, not the least of which was a guy named Steve Young. He went on to become an All-Pro quarterback and a Super Bowl MVP leading the San Francisco 49ers. We were the decided underdogs, but I liked our chances.

My belief was not unfounded. As the fourth quarter ticked down, we were just four points behind with two minutes left to play. Earlier in the season, no one would ever have imagined we'd be in that position, but there we were, putting the league's leading team on their heels. The only belief that mattered was ours.

We were sixty-five yards away from the end zone and needed a touchdown. With a minute and forty seconds left and no timeouts, we began our drive. A few short passes picked up a couple of first downs, then we found ourselves facing fourth and ten.

In any normal situation, our offensive coordinator would have called the play, but given the stakes, he turned to me with a look that said, *Give me some direction here!* He was the first person I'd hired after becoming head coach. After more than fifty years in college and the NFL, he'd retired to San Diego, but he took a break from retirement when he got my call. He'd been integral in getting us this far, and I didn't want him to have to live with his decision if things didn't go our way, so I took it upon myself to make the call.

I went with a running play. It went against all logic not to go with a pass, given the setup, but I decided on a handoff to our star running back. When the quarterback got word of the play, he stood up from the huddle and looked at me. "Are you shitting me?" he yelled.

"Just run the goddamn play," I barked.

The reason I'd called a run was that during the last three plays, we'd been under heavy pressure from blitzes. I didn't want the game to end with our quarterback on his back, having no chance to make a play.

My bet was right. At the snap, the defense came in hard on the middle of our line. Our star running back got perfect blocking, enabling him to run a sweep away from the center. When he turned the corner, there was nothing in front of him but daylight.

The Express had an extremely fast defensive back, and because he had an angle, he was able to take down our back at the four-yard line. There were twenty seconds on the clock—enough for two plays.

On the first play, there were no open receivers, so our quarterback threw the ball away. We were down to the last play, and the entire season was on the line.

The quarterback targeted our tight end, who was open about four yards into the end zone. At the last moment, a linebacker tipped the ball just enough to nudge its trajectory from the center of the intended receiver's chest to just above his shoulder. While the receiver was able to readjust enough to stop the ball, he couldn't catch it. It was the end of the game, our Cinderella story, and our hallelujahs.

When I entered the locker room, I was prepared to see a group of beleaguered men with their heads held low. Down, dejected, perhaps even angry. But the reality was the opposite. It was as if, in that moment, instead of focusing on what they had lost in a few brief moments, they realized what they'd gained over the season. All the ridicule they'd endured, the self-doubt, the adversity and uncertainty they'd overcome were at the forefront of their minds, and they were rightfully proud. Yes, in the end, we'd lost the game, but over the longer arc of the season, they had proven themselves, and they knew they were coming away from the experience as winners. They'd learned a lesson I had internalized myself during college: Sometimes, the greatest victories are not reflected in the score.

Together, we joined in a triumphant chorus of eight hallelujahs. They'd earned it.

With the end of the season came the end of my tenure as head coach. Halfway through the season, the owner had announced that he'd hired a permanent head coach who would take over when the season ended, effectively leaving me a lame duck. He'd had little faith in my ability to lead the team and overlooked my prediction about our early losses eventually giving way to wins. In a bid to preserve the fan base and prevent them from giving up on us, he hired a well-known coach from the Oakland Raiders who would stand in wait to take my place.

I was invited to interview for other head-coaching positions within the league, but I was reluctant to do so. It wasn't due to a lack of desire or confidence, but because I believed I saw the writing on the wall for the USFL, and it wasn't good.

The first two years were like proof of concept for the league. Fans were indeed glad for a spring football option, and I think that could have continued. Yet as I feared, the USFL's worst enemy was itself. In the second year, the league added several new teams, and the New Jersey Generals were acquired by a real estate mogul by the name of Donald Trump. Trump's vision for the league was to shift to the fall, where it would be a direct competitor with the NFL, and he pushed hard for it. My decision, therefore, was not about whether I should interview for coaching positions, but whether I should stay in the league at all. The way I saw it, the USFL's days could be numbered, and if that happened, there'd be a deluge of coaches on the market. Unemployment lines would suddenly be filled with ex-USFL employees.

Once again, my relationship with Forrest Gregg came into play. We'd stayed in touch since our Toronto days, and he was now the head coach of the Green Bay Packers. They were searching for someone to replace their current contract negotiator—a skill with which I now had significant experience. Forrest recommended me to the search committee. Several weeks later, they offered me the job with a start date of January 5, 1986.

But before I left for Green Bay, I had other business to attend to—business of a more personal nature. As it turned out, I'd be shouting "Hallelujah" about a few other things as well.

CHAPTER 12

A New Day

During my first year in Oakland, I had no personal life to speak of. Getting the team off the ground took all my focus, and that was okay with me. Any free time would have been filled with thoughts of my boys, so as far as I was concerned, it was better to just stay busy.

The owner of the Invaders didn't think much of my approach to life. He was friends with a woman named Eileen, who was in the process of getting a divorce, and as it turned out, she'd gone to Ohio State as well. He thought we had a lot in common and arranged for us to have a casual meeting after a team event.

From the moment I met Eileen, I was interested, but it was one-sided. That was fair enough, as it turned out that having gone to OSU was just about the only thing we had in common. She had no interest at all in football; she didn't know whether a ball was blown or stuffed. While at school, she'd been into studying and pot, and I knew very little about either. Still, she had an overall appeal that attracted me. For starters, she was striking, and her looks were matched with a sophistication and elegance that I found compelling. She dressed impeccably, and it was clear to me even from our brief encounter that she was a class act. Then there was me. Next to her, I felt like a knuckle-dragger—and I basically was—but I figured I would give it a shot anyway.

Trying to play it cool, I waited about a week before I reached out to ask if she'd like to go out. "I'm busy," she said. I waited a bit, then tried again. In response to every date I suggested, I got the same reply: "I'm busy" or "That won't work for me."

Finally I said, "Okay, well, why don't you tell me a day that might be good for you." Lo and behold, after several weeks of near begging on my part, Eileen eventually agreed to have dinner with me.

Wanting to make a good impression, I got done up in my finest: my best jeans, a long-sleeve white linen shirt, lizard-skin cowboy boots, and to really make her take notice, my favorite Western belt, along with my signature John Deere belt buckle. As the guys on the football team would have said, I was "all the way live."

When I showed up on her doorstep in my finery, Eileen put on her best poker face, trying to disguise her reaction. Later, she confided that it took some real willpower not to tell me she felt a twenty-four-hour flu coming on and would have to cancel. Fortunately for me, she was willing to look past my sartorial ineptitude. It was country mouse meets city mouse. I told myself I'd better enjoy the date, because it was sure to be a one-and-done situation.

Eileen took me to the Balboa Cafe in the marina district for burgers, fries, and beer. As far as I was concerned, that was starting things out on the right foot. She was an executive for a direct-marketing company, and she obviously knew her business. I loved her independence and drive. As the evening wore on, I learned that we had a few things in common after all. Maybe not so much in terms of externals, but as we talked, it became more and more evident that on a deeper level, something clicked. We had dinner that Friday night, and I said goodbye on Sunday.

Still, as I was leaving, Eileen told me flat out not to get any ideas. She had a full life between work and friends and wouldn't be going out of her way to carve out space for me. It was a good four to six weeks before I finally saw her again. From there, we continued to see each other off and on. During the season, I often had little notice as to when I would be free, so when I called, she often wasn't available. I was interested in more, but then my priorities suddenly shifted.

I got a call from Ann, who'd been in a serious car accident where she was at fault. The driver was killed, and the passenger was badly injured. The boys had been in the car with Ann but mercifully weren't hurt. The incident was getting a lot of local media attention, and to Ann's credit, she was worried about how all of it would affect the boys. She wanted to send them to come live with me.

We were a week away from the opening game of the season, my first with the Invaders. Two days before, the team's sports director and I had rented a home and moved in together. It was a two-bedroom condo and therefore not big enough to accommodate two young boys. Once again, a group of friends saved me by leaping into action.

Among my angels were my friends in Cleveland who I had stayed with during my short stint in Ohio after being let go by the Argonauts. They offered to fly out with the boys and help get them settled. They ended up staying on for two weeks until I was able to hire a nanny.

I also received immediate and immense support from the Invaders' executive front-office administrator and her family. Between her, her husband, and their two daughters, they found us a place to live, furnished it, and helped us move in. They also opened their home to us anytime we wanted to visit. It was like an instant family.

There were other helpers, too. The local car dealer who provided cars for the Invaders' staff found out about my predicament and loaned me a car that would be suitable for a Mr. Mom.

Thanks to an abundance of friendship and charity from others, when the boys arrived, they not only had a nicely appointed home to come to but were even enrolled in school. When they got off the plane and I saw their beautiful faces, it was truly one of the happiest days of my life. Once again, it was all thanks to an abundance of generosity from others—people who had not only the inclination to jump in and assist but also the skills and resources to do so in the way I needed.

Some people struggle to ask for help. Others have no issue seeking help but do so in the wrong places. Whether it's self-help, personal help, family help, help with health issues, and so on, they might have the right questions, but they're asking the wrong people. When this happens, it's easy to internalize the outcome and believe it's a reflection on them—a sign that they simply can't be helped. But often I think it's more about looking to the wrong sources or just asking for the wrong things. Sometimes we're not clear about what we need, so we go to people who can't effectively help us. It comes back to that idea of getting really clear about your priorities and what you need, so you know who to ask and how they can help.

Ultimately, so much about the quality of life comes down to the relationships you make with other people. These friends were the salt of the earth. They were the type of people I wanted to associate with, period, and so I put real effort into my relationships with them. As a result, I didn't have trouble asking for their help. If you only cultivate connections because of what others might do for you, that's using people. But if you foster genuine relationships with people who have similar visions, beliefs, and values—people who view the world and others much the same way you do—those are the people who will never let you down. They'll be there when you need something, just like you'll be there for them.

Just like in Canada, a collection of kind folks saved our lives. I don't want to even think of where the kids and I would have been without them. As it was, we didn't miss a beat. The Monday after the boys arrived, they went to school and I went to practice.

As the boys and I found our new groove, Eileen and I started seeing more of each other. She was totally open to the idea that I was now a single dad, and the four of us started spending time together. We'd go into the city some weekends and play tourist while Eileen took us to parks and museums. Getting to be with both the boys and Eileen felt absolutely perfect. Unfortunately, my fairy tale was about to end.

"We need to talk," Eileen called and told me. She'd been thinking about it, and she'd decided to give her marriage one last try. Her husband was moving to New York for work, and she was going with him.

I couldn't believe what I was hearing. I accepted her decision. After all, what choice did I have? But as I hung up the phone, I was devastated. I went over to the apartment of the friends who'd introduced us and told them what had happened. I remember falling back against their wall and then just sliding down onto the floor. I sat there and bawled my eyes out.

Then, unimaginably, things got even worse.

While the boys and I were living our lives, Ann, my now ex-wife, had moved within two hours of San Francisco, where she entered a drug-treatment program. After she was released, she petitioned the court for custody of the boys. Once again, her petition was granted. At the time, if a woman could prove that she was a child's mother and there was no obvious evidence of abuse or neglect, regardless of any past behavior or legal infractions, she would get custody.

I didn't even know she was in California, but suddenly there she was on our doorstep, flanked by two police officers. She'd told them she feared for her safety, so they'd accompanied her. Just like that, once again, my boys were gone.

My life had become a real-life version of the movie *Kramer vs. Kramer*. In it, Meryl Streep leaves Dustin Hoffman and their son. Then, fifteen months later, she returns and files for custody, which she's given. I deeply identified with the confusion and anguish Hoffman's character experienced. He'd been a reliable father who had poured his love into his son, but in the eyes of the law, that didn't matter.

Sadly for all of us, this scenario was repeated multiple times. Ann would be in and out of rehab, sometimes after scrapes with the law. The boys would come back to me, but as soon as she was released, she'd once again be granted custody. Wash, rinse, repeat. It was painful for me, but the worst part was knowing what my sons were having to endure, getting bounced back and forth between their parents. I just wanted them to have a loving, stable home, and I knew that given the setup, that would be with me.

This wasn't the only roller coaster I was on. During Eileen's time in New York, she called me about twice a week. Obviously, the reconciliation wasn't working out. She decided to move back to San Francisco, yet she made it clear that she wasn't moving back for me. She simply knew that she didn't want to be married anymore.

Then, after an Invaders game, Eileen called and asked if I'd like to go out for dinner. I said no. I wasn't too pleased with her declaration that she hadn't come back for me, and I wasn't sure how I felt about our prospects. Truth be told, I was simply worn out. My heart was so weary I wasn't sure that I could handle being that vulnerable again. Plus, I'd become the head coach, and without my sons around, the team was my highest priority.

It was one of the times in life when I put my work above all else. There have been periods when I've even put work before my family, at least in terms of the hours I devoted to it. But I did that consciously and for good reason. I was making a short-term commitment of my time and energy to net a long-term gain for my family. I reasoned that a solid career wouldn't benefit only me; it would provide the kind of stability and security I wanted for them. Still, when you work late or miss an event, it can be hard to justify it to others—to explain to your kids or your wife that you're actually doing it to benefit the big picture. It's like giving up the good for the great, or making short-term sacrifices for long-term gains.

At that point, I needed to pour my attention into the job at hand. After all, we had a season to turn around. I wasn't going to overlook the promise I'd made to my players to do everything in my power to help them succeed.

Now that I wasn't as available, Eileen was the one pursuing me. Granted, she didn't beg me like I'd begged her, but eventually I did agree to see her. When we finally got together, it was like something shifted. Perhaps it was that she finally had closure on her marriage. In any event, from then on, we were pretty much inseparable. It was finally clear that we were going somewhere.

Eileen and I had our challenges, but when you have the kind of relationship where you hold the same values and beliefs, you build a trust that's undeniable. In some ways, she and I were as different as champagne and beer, but we trusted one another implicitly. Still, I'm sure that plenty of people found our partnership puzzling. But what was most important to Eileen was being with someone who would be there for her no matter what. She knew that if I committed to something, it was as good as done. For my part, in addition to Eileen's independence, I appreciated her determination and the diverse interests she cultivated. Before I met her, I had never even attended a theatrical production. She broadened my world.

I knew I wasn't going to find someone better for me, because there was no such person. Eileen was it. That was a lesson I'd learned from my first marriage. I had jumped into that relationship without any real understanding of what to look for in a partner. That mistake helped me to recognize a true, deep connection when I found it. The more time Eileen and I spent together, the more our strengths as a couple became even stronger.

When I got the offer to join the Green Bay Packers, Eileen and I had known each other for about two and a half years. There was no question I wanted her to come with me to Green Bay. When I asked her, she looked at me plainly and said, "Not unless we're married."

That was fine with me, but there was one other small detail we'd need to sort out, which was life in Green Bay. It was not the bay area that Eileen was used to. With its long, frigid winters, it was a far cry from San Francisco. And while the town now has a lot going for it, let's just say that the Green Bay of today has come a long way since the mid-eighties.

I went ahead and moved, and a few weeks later, Eileen came out to visit and get a feel for the place. It was deep in the heart of winter—we figured that she deserved to get the full picture before making a decision. She needed to experience not only the culture of Green Bay but also the weather.

I was at the airport, waiting to pick up Eileen, when I struck up a conversation with a guy who was there to pick up his wife. As it happened, he owned one of the largest advertising agencies in Green Bay. I mentioned that Eileen was in marketing and that I was hoping she'd soon be my wife, and therefore would be looking for a job in town. "Have her call me," he said. He was smart enough to recognize an opportunity when he saw it. At that time, it wasn't every day that someone with Eileen's talent and experience landed in Green Bay.

Upon Eileen's arrival, we checked in to the best hotel in town: the Ramada Inn. I took her to the lounge so we could have a drink before dinner. Wine was her beverage of choice, and during her time in California, she often took advantage of her proximity to its legendary vineyards with their endless selection of fine wines.

When the waitress arrived, Eileen asked what kinds of wine were available. "We have a Riesling and a Chablis," the waitress said, beaming. To Eileen, it was like being invited to choose between death by gunshot or stabbing. She chose stabbing.

When the waitress returned, her tray held not only my beer but also two twelve-ounce tumblers brimming with Chablis. When Eileen asked about the portion size, the waitress beamed once more. "It's a special. It's Double Bubble!" Eileen laughed with her and offered a cheers. Then she looked at me and said, "I guess we're not in Kansas anymore." I heard wedding bells.

During the visit, the weather was clear and sunny. Eileen called the advertising exec I'd met at the airport and went in for an interview. He offered her a job on the spot. We found a home under construction and decided to buy it. Everything was coming together even more smoothly than I could have hoped.

Two months later, Eileen and I were married in a small ceremony at a friend's home in Orinda, California. The boys were there and served as my best men.

The wedding was not without some unexpected excitement. For one, I made the mistake of giving Brady, my youngest, Eileen's ring to hold on to until the ceremony. He and his brother were playing outside, and when I asked him where the ring was, he realized he'd lost it. Fortunately, after some frantic searching, we found it just in time.

The other episode of note—beyond our vows, that is—was the excitement generated by one of the guests. The attorney for the Invaders was in attendance and brought as his date a woman who'd been a Playboy Playmate of the Year. At a wedding, it's poor form to pay too much attention to any woman other than the bride, but those guys couldn't help themselves. I'm certain half the photos that were taken that day were not of our wedding.

Afterward, Eileen joined me in Green Bay, and we moved into our new home. The dust was still settling from our move when I got a call from one of my ex-wife's friends. She told me that Ann had overdosed and was in bad shape. The boys were there at her house and had no money. I needed to come get them. I was on the next flight out.

I retrieved the boys and took them to a friend's house in the city, where we stayed overnight while I got them sorted out. I cleaned them up and bought them clothes and some other basics, then we flew back to Green Bay. Within a matter of days, Eileen had become both a wife and a mom to stepsons ages eight and ten, and she was delighted.

After so many stints in rehab and brushes with the law, Ann's luck with the courts had finally run out. To all involved, it was now undeniable that the best place for the boys was with me. Even Ann knew it. In an act of true love, which must have been absolutely excruciating, she gave up her fight for custody and permanently released the boys into my care.

In the previous years, I had endured the lowest lows a man

can experience. Fortunately, I'd had enough support to get me through. My sons had experienced their own trials. But now all of that was done. A new day had finally dawned, and we were free to be a family.

CHAPTER 13

The Calm After the Storm

When the Packers' season started, I had to travel with the team. I felt a little uneasy being away from home so often, with all the changes our family had just experienced. It seemed a lot to ask of Eileen. When I was on the road, each time I was about to return home, I had a vision of walking into the house and seeing a message written in lipstick on the mirror. "Honey, I tried. . . . I'm outta here." Fortunately, it never happened.

I knew that being a lone caregiver wasn't easy, but somehow Eileen managed it beautifully. She knew just the tone to take with the boys. From day one, she told them, "I'm not here to replace your mother, but I am here to be your best friend." As challenging as the situation was for all of us, it was one of the most rewarding experiences in my life to watch our family come together.

For her part, one of Eileen's main objectives was to have the boys learn to be independent, so she taught them how to cook, how to do their laundry, and so on. She'd say to both of them, "You'll be a great husband to someone someday." She and the boys would watch the cooking channels together, and to this day, they all still love to cook. They'll exchange recipes and talk about great meals they've had. It's a far cry from my days swapping meal tips with moms at the PTA meetings.

When it came to my parenting role, I had one objective: Every decision I made would be in their best interest. Whether it was emotionally or physically, their well-being came first. I wanted to do the very best I could for them, given what they'd gone through. It wasn't their fault that their parents weren't together and that their mother was struggling. As much as possible, I wanted to minimize the impact that had on them as they grew up.

It helped that from the time they were born, I was fully present in their lives. Because of Ann's unstable situation, I had taken the night feedings. I was the one who took them to the doctor. When it came down to it, there wasn't anything I hadn't done or wasn't comfortable doing.

At the same time, I didn't have a magic wand. I knew there was only so much I could do, and their situation was still a difficult one. It was important to acknowledge that, but to also frame it in a way so that, hopefully, they wouldn't feel permanently disadvantaged by it.

I told them that everything they'd gone through—being exposed to addiction, going back and forth between households, and sometimes living in unstable situations—all of it had forced them to grow up sooner than they should have. I acknowledged that they missed out on some aspects of childhood they should have gotten to experience. At the same time, in the long run, they would also benefit from those experiences. "You're going to feel the negatives now," I told them, "but at some point, you'll also see that there are positives. You'll have a set of skills and a resilience that will serve you as you learn how to apply them." My job was to make sure they got through childhood without incurring so many scars that they wouldn't be able to see those benefits later. There is good to be found in everything; sometimes you just need to look a little harder.

When you're in a situation with your family where you've faced extreme challenges, you're compelled to have a lot of difficult conversations. If you want to make it through instead of falling apart, you have to have continual dialogue with your kids. They're emotional and they're confused, and it's up to you to help them work through it. Even when they were with me and Eileen, there was still nothing completely normal or stable about their lives, because they were still worried about their mother. They had a lot more on their minds than most kids their age.

All this required me to build muscles that, up to then, were relatively weak. I wasn't naturally communicative, and often I was reluctant to express my feelings. But I had to find a way to be open and honest with the boys. It was a difficult balance, because while I had to be understanding and sympathetic, I was also the dad. I had to be the enforcer as well as the protector and nurturer. When I grew up, it was "Either my way or the highway!"

While I tried to strike a balance in my own behavior between sympathy and stoicism, I also tried to foster that in the boys. I felt it was important for them to get a sense of their emotional boundaries. It was perfectly fine to want care and sympathy, yet at some point, it was time to take a breath, steady yourself, and move on. The consistency in that variation is critical. We all need to learn when we've reached that end point on either side; otherwise, we can overindulge and start to feel sorry for ourselves, or we can go the other way and shut down. There's no formula for teaching that or for learning it—in my experience, it's all instinct. For me, it came down to having the right objective, the right vision, and the right outcome in mind, and then sensing and feeling where

I was trying to go. It's not easy, but you figure out how to get there along the way. Maybe the best rule of thumb is to do all you can to resolve things on your own, then ask for help.

One hard-and-fast rule was that I tried never to let my sons go to bed upset. There were plenty of times they were out of sorts, either because they upset themselves or I upset them, but I always went to their room before they fell asleep and tried to make them feel better. It didn't always work, but it was important to me to let them know it was all going to be okay. We had to have that dialogue even if it was just saying "Good night, I love you." I didn't want them going to bed wondering what would happen. They could be mad at me, but they needed to know I loved them and I'd still be there for them in the morning.

I don't know how good a job I did. I can tell you that I couldn't be prouder of who my sons have become, but I don't know how much credit I can take for that. What I *can* say is I did my best. And I can also say that the evolution of our family as it came together is one of the happiest, proudest things I've ever experienced.

Fortunately, my work with the Packers provided clearer metrics. The team had hired me with a goal of reducing their payroll. The problem was they'd been overpaying for average ball players. When I was with the USFL, I saw how players' agents would play one league against the other. When it came to the NFL, the agents called Green Bay "the candy store," because it was so easy to get what they wanted. The trouble was, they weren't getting the results to justify their big payouts and were not receiving high-caliber performances.

I was indebted to Forrest because he got me that first interview, but he didn't recommend me because he wanted a yes-man. He did it because he knew my skill set, and he knew I could be relied on to do my job. I didn't just green-light everything the coaches wanted; my true value was that I knew what Forrest and the team needed to be successful.

When I played for the Browns, it was crushing to have experienced ongoing problems with injuries. My dream of a long, productive career as a player in the NFL was over. At the same time, another opportunity presented itself.

I could have just stayed back in the locker room, doing my rehab, and no one would have questioned it, but I wanted to be more involved. I was still part of the team, and I wanted to make some kind of contribution. As a result, Forrest essentially made me an associate coach. I sat in on all the coaches' meetings, where I gave what was essentially a scouting report on every player we were going to go up against. At the beginning of every Monday morning meeting, as we looked forward to our next opponent, I had the floor for at least thirty minutes to critique the other team's players and the opponent's overall strengths and weaknesses. It was invaluable experience and exposure.

When I landed back in the NFL, this time in the front office, I realized that had I never sought out that role while I was injured, I never would have been exposed to Forrest in that way. He never would have seen what else I could do. It was proof to me that if you do the right things and you do them to the best of your ability, you can make something worthwhile out of an undesirable situation. Things might not work out in the time frame you want them to, but over time, they will work out. Sometimes, you need to trust life. To simply believe that doing the right thing, at the right time, in the right way will net a positive result, even if you have no idea when that will be.

From my earliest days, my father had instilled in me the idea that you should always do your best. Now, I was deepening my understanding of why. When you turn in your best effort at whatever you're asked to do, not only will it come back and benefit you later, but you will also live a life without regrets. You'll never be in that situation of wondering what might have happened if only you'd applied yourself more. If only you'd taken advantage of that opportunity.

My overall objective as the Packers' negotiator was to sign players for what they were worth.

We had several players who'd made All-Pro within the last three to four years but who were no longer playing at that level. The fans loved them, but less so the people cutting their paychecks. My job was to balance the payroll, which included balancing the team and their performance and paying everyone accordingly. I called it "pay-for-play."

As part of that task, the coaching staff and I agreed that we needed to find guys who were playing better than our lackluster All-Pros. When their contracts were up, I offered them a salary commensurate with their play and incentives on the back end of the contract to make up for the difference in their pay. The players were displeased, to say the least, as were their agents, who made their money based on salaried pay, not incentives. In the end, I released the overpaid players, some of whom ended up signing with other teams for less money than I'd offered. The other players retired.

Throughout the NFL, most of my counterparts on other teams were attorneys. I didn't have that kind of legal experience, but I was a fast learner, and I had common sense. Plus, the USFL had been the perfect classroom. From that experience, I knew something about each of the agents and how they operated, and that information was invaluable. I was also confident in my ability to understand what a player was worth. My experience as a coach gave me that advantage over both the attorneys and the agents.

One of the most important things I learned in Oakland was that favorable negotiations were the product of good preparation. You have to know what things you absolutely must have, along with your walking-away price, before you even start. You need that kind of clarity to guide the process; trying to figure it out in the middle of a negotiation is too late.

Failing in a negotiation because you failed to prepare goes under the category of beating yourself. Poor or inadequate preparation can set us up to lose before we even begin. Sometimes we're overconfident, thinking we know it all or it won't be that hard. Or maybe you know your side, but have failed to consider the other side. I've seen people prepare presentations without considering how the audience or the customer will receive the information and what their experience will be. Or they don't anticipate what could go wrong or the questions that might be asked.

Preparation is the hard part, but it's worth the energy. Executing becomes fun and even easy when you've put in sufficient effort up front. And whatever you're doing, enjoyment is important. If executing isn't fun, then something's seriously wrong, and most often, you can attribute it to a lack of preparation. Unfortunately, I don't think many people are willing to dedicate the energy it really takes to fully prepare. But if you do, then you will certainly distinguish yourself, and you'll have a lot more fun in the process.

Typically, I went into a negotiation offering between 80 and 85 percent of where I was willing to go. I wanted the player and their agent to know I respected them. In my view, lowballing served no purpose and could be detrimental to the process. Why create hard feelings at the outset?

A lot of negotiating comes down to people skills and whether you can read and understand the other party. Some think it's all about money, but everyone is motivated by different things. You need to understand what moves people and what's actually important to them. You also need to know something about who you're negotiating against.

Another essential element of dealmaking is timing. You need to have a sense of when to make that final offer or push. Of when to pull out that ace card—to offer them something you know is going to get their attention and make them budge. I discovered it's not always so much about what that thing is, but about when you offer it.

People have asked me what's the best deal I ever made. I always tell them it's the deal I *didn't* make. Sometimes, you have to walk away, but if you've executed the process well, at that point, that's a good thing. It means walking away was the right thing. Sometimes, that's a successful negotiation, because you dodged a bullet.

There's no set formula for what a winning negotiation looks like. People will always love to look back after the paperwork is signed and say you should have done this or that. It's easy to second-guess whether you could have gotten them for less or otherwise made out better on your end. But as the people doing the negotiating know, the process has so many moving parts, and each negotiation is unique. That's one of the benefits of being absolutely clear at the outset about your nonnegotiables and your must-haves. If you've gotten what you need, and you haven't caved on any of your nonnegotiables, then it's a success. You don't have to second-guess yourself. Plus, there's value in not creating hard feelings during the process if you don't have to. Perhaps you might have gotten someone to sign for less, but if they don't feel good about the deal, they'll carry that into the relationship.

By those metrics, I made a lot of successful deals for the Packers, but some outside the front office did not think so. Most days, the fans, the players—maybe even the whole city of Green Bay—wanted to have me for lunch. That was fine, but what bothered me was when my kids were harassed at school. It wasn't pretty. It was hard to escape it, because it seemed like every day, some agent was in the paper, complaining that I was doing a lousy job. They'd say that I was in over my head and I didn't know how to negotiate.

I never commented, because it was my belief that when it came to the papers, you couldn't have a one-sided argument. I'd get to work at 6 a.m. and there would be four reporters at my door, waiting for me. My response was always the same: "I'm not negotiating in the paper. What goes on is privileged between the agents, the players, and me." It drove the reporters crazy, but I'd been in the business long enough to know where a back-and-forth in the papers led, and it was nowhere good. There was nothing about it that would benefit my negotiations in any way. Instead, it would just become a "he said, she said," and that would have taken me away from my objective, which was to get the player signed.

After my four years working for the Packers, we became the twentieth-highest-paying team in the league while retaining nearly the same record. What I'd done was to set the table for the next person to take my spot. They now had money to work with to build a stronger team. Forrest was in a position to sign free agents and get better players. I'd done my job. I'd been the bad guy, and the way I saw it, it was time for someone else to take it from there.

The CEO, the executive committee, and Forrest all seemed happy with the work I'd done and wanted me to keep doing it as long as I was interested. I was offered a lifetime contract. For many—perhaps most—in my position, the potential for a lifetime position with the Packers would have been a dream come true. Yet for me, it was actually a disincentive.

I'd become just as comfortable and confident as a negotiator as I was as a coach. Yet while each negotiation was different and each situation new, my learning curve had flattened too much for my liking. I know lots of people seek that horizon—they're excited to arrive at the place where things are no longer so challenging, where you can show up at work, get your coffee, and just roll through your day. To me, that sounded a lot like dying.

Once again, I recalled one of Woody's philosophies: "You're either getting better or worse; you never stay the same." For me, there was no such thing as status quo, and since I didn't see a lot more room where I could improve or areas where there was more to learn, that spelled a steady decline. Sure, I could be more efficient and tune the dial to get a little bit better here and there, but I wasn't going to expand my knowledge base in any significant way.

When I looked beyond my own position to the rest of the front office, there was some appeal to potentially becoming a general manager or a VP of operations. But I knew with the limited exposure I'd had, that wasn't going to happen in the time frame I wanted it to.

I had just turned forty and felt like I was going to have to go one way or the other. Either settle into a relatively cushy position where I wasn't really learning and wasn't particularly challenged, or do something completely different. The way I saw it, if I didn't make a big change then, I doubted I ever would. With that thought in mind, I tendered my resignation.

It was time to start over, but just like when I left the NFL as a player, I had no idea where.

I did have some sense of what kind of role I wanted to try. My enjoyment and passion came from using my strongest skills. If I could use my skills with people, leadership, negotiating, and teamwork, along with my mental toughness, I would have been fine making widgets.

The idea of sales appealed to me. Some people didn't see the line from football to sales, but to me, there were obvious parallels. I would have clear goals and objectives, I could control my own destiny, and I could see where I was at all times; plus I could leverage my strengths.

There were plenty of jobs in sales out there, but I knew I couldn't land just anywhere. At my age, and with a family to consider, I didn't have room to make a mistake. And I didn't have four or five years to waste figuring out that I'd made a bad choice. I needed to land at a solid company where I'd have the opportunity to advance quickly, because I knew I'd be starting at the bottom. It was just a matter of finding that place.

When I began to think of the world outside football, the potential opportunities became endless. It felt like I was searching for the proverbial needle in a haystack. In the past, I realized in retrospect that I'd gotten lucky—the moves I'd made had ended up working out, yet I didn't see in the moment how high the stakes had been. This time, I knew damn well. By my calculations, I had one shot to get it right.

CHAPTER 14

Farewell to Football

While working for the Packers, I became friends with two of my neighbors. As it happened, both were senior vice presidents for the same privately held food-service company. One led retail sales, and the other ran food-service sales. I told them about my decision to change careers, and they both thought I might be an asset to their company, Schreiber Foods.

Schreiber is the largest private-label manufacturer of cheese in the United States. Their customers comprised grocery stores, fast-food restaurants, and food-service distributors. At the time, they had sixteen plants, six thousand partners, and annual sales totaling more than $400 million.

I was interviewed by several officers, the board of directors, and eventually the CEO, whom I knew because he was a member of the Packers' board of directors. As I advanced through their interview process, I observed what Schreiber was like as a company—its culture and values.

In the end, I accepted a position as an entry-level sales rep, selling to food-service distributors in Northern California.

Still, my decision was not an easy one. The other new hires filling such positions were recent college graduates. I would be taking a forty-thousand-dollar pay cut and relocating my family back to the Bay Area. We were settled in Green Bay by then. We had our house, the boys felt at home there, and Eileen was happy in her role at the advertising agency. In addition to leaving all we had built, we'd be moving to one of the most expensive areas in the country at a time when mortgage interest rates were upward of 13 percent.

My decision came down to three things. First, the CEO agreed that as I proved myself, I would be fast-tracked for advancement. The second was the demonstrated values and beliefs of the company's partners, especially the senior leaders. I believe that an organization is a direct reflection of its leadership. If it is right at the top, it is right at the bottom, and I liked what I saw. Finally, I could have a great impact in determining my future—as with my football career, input would determine output.

Now, it was up to me. The reason I'd chosen sales was that I saw it as essentially an individual sport. The bar would be whatever I wanted to set it at, and I wanted it high. All I needed was the CEO's assurance that my future depended on me and my performance, and I had that. My destiny was in my own hands.

To that point, every significant move in my life and my career stemmed from another person choosing to become my benefactor. When I was in high school, the county judge reached out to tell Woody about me. When I got the job in Toronto, it was because of Forrest. My old colleague John Ralston reached out to hire me in Oakland. Forrest reappeared and recommended me to Green Bay. And now, my neighbors and friends recommended me to Schreiber Foods. I firmly believe that when you consistently do your best, others will notice. When you establish meaningful relationships with people on top of that, they're even more likely to consider you, should future opportunities arise. Quality people want to associate themselves with quality people.

Relationships expand the potential for opportunities to become available to you. That's not news. We know that networking is powerful. The problem is that these days, people want the connection and the recommendation without an actual relationship. They're happy to reach out and connect with someone only for the purpose of trying to advance themselves. It's transactional. The kind of relationships I'm talking about are authentic. They're a natural by-product of the trust and goodwill you build with others when you show up consistently and do good work. That kind of street credit simply can't be bought—it must be earned.

The first six months at Schreiber were a trial by fire. When I joined the company, I would have felt more comfortable being in a management position than in entry-level sales. It didn't help that Schreiber didn't have the most robust training program. It was a bit of a hodgepodge. I spent a few weeks in the plant, then was sent to spend time with this person or that person, each of whom could show me bits and pieces of what I needed to know.

Something that was especially useful was spending two weeks in the middle of winter at Schreiber's plant in Logan, Utah, home to Utah State University. The plant and the Utes were the two largest employers in the area (and their employees occupied the majority of the dining establishments, which is how I came by that information). My housing on that trip was a motel—the kind with plastic cups in the rooms, a coin-operated massage bed, an outdoor Coke machine, and a breakfast waitress who greeted me each morning at 5 a.m. with a "Hi, honey." Best of all, due to a lack of a proper seal, a perfectly formed snow castle materialized inside my room every day. What more could a former Green Bay Packers executive wish for?

But despite such colorful and fairly edifying experiences, I realized the only way I was going to truly learn the position was out in the field. I asked them to cut me loose and let me learn the rest on the job, so they moved me back to San Francisco.

I spent the next year traveling around to various accounts. To add to the challenge, the company hadn't had a salesperson in my territory for the last five years. Many customers were still purchasing from us, but the relationships had gone largely untended. The customers' loyalty said a lot about the quality of our products but little about how the company valued them. Often, when I met with clients, I would hear comments such as "So *this* is what a Schreiber salesperson looks like!" and, even worse, "So why do we need you?" But the most humbling incident took place at a food show in Fresno.

It was July, which in Fresno is Africa hot. The daytime high got well over one hundred, which at night dropped only into the lower eighties. The conditions were terrible, but attendance was part of the job. A food show is an opportunity for companies to display their products to current and potential customers. Suppliers set up booths in large exhibition halls and then endure two grueling days—picture eleven-hour days standing on a cement floor, talking about cheese. All this was done essentially in support of a larger food distributor, so it made little direct impact on my business. It was, as they say, a long run for a short slide. But I was committed to representing Schreiber well.

Hoping to avoid both the crowds and the heat, I showed up about ninety minutes before the exhibition hall opened. After consulting the show map, I located my booth and started to set up my samples, which had come via overnight delivery from one of our plants. With my display all set up, I had a good hour to spare. Time to catch my breath and relax until showtime. That was, until the woman at the booth next to me spoke up.

Her display was of cleaning supplies and equipment, and it was immediately evident that she had a lot more experience than I. "Hey, what's going on with that bag?" she asked, pointing to a package of shredded cheese. "It looks like it's about to burst. That doesn't seem normal, does it?" I wasn't sure, but being a rookie, I was inclined to take her advice. I put in a call to my customer-service rep in Green Bay and described the bag in question.

"Yes, that's a problem," she said. When I'd unpacked the samples, I hadn't questioned the lack of cooling agents in the boxes. There'd been nothing with the cheese to keep it sufficiently cold. The result was a five-pound yellow balloon.

"What can I do?" I asked.

Since it was too late for them to send new samples, my only option was to head to a local distributor to retrieve products from their inventory—a thirty-minute drive away. When I got back, I had the new samples in tow, but by that time, the parking lot looked like a football game five minutes before kickoff. I had to park nearly a mile away.

I made it just before the show started, but it was like my freshman biology midterm all over again. I had to spend the entire morning soaked in my own perspiration. When the show was over, I trashed my clothes. But there was a highlight. At the close of the event, my new friend from the cleaning-supplies booth gave me a push broom to commemorate my inauguration into the food-show scene. Nearly forty years later, I'm still sweeping my garage with that broom, and I'll never forget how I came by it.

In spite of a challenging start, my performance was solid and put me in a position to take advantage of an opportunity, should one present itself. Fortunately, and as promised by the CEO, I didn't have long to wait before one appeared.

I'd been working as a district manager reporting to the western regional manager. My boss oversaw not only me but also four other district managers who worked part-time covering sixteen states. He'd handpicked each of them, and when I met them, it was evident why. All of them were very attractive women, which was clearly part of his concept of client service. It was self-serving as well. He would visit each territory and, under the guise of attending to the customers, go along and make a few sales calls with the managers, then take them to lunch, dinner, even drinks. I knew all these women because we were peers, and I knew most of them just weren't that good at their jobs. That's not to say that attractive women can't also make excellent sales reps, but as I learned from working with them, few among this group had the dedication to match their looks.

Leadership was similarly unhappy with my boss's results, and about a year into my tenure, he was fired. Later, I learned that I'd been hired with the idea that I might someday become his replacement, and that's exactly what happened.

From previous experience, I knew that winning requires the right team. You win with people if they are the right people, and you lose if they're not. When I took over as western regional manager, I knew I'd have to make some staffing changes. With one exception, the women who now reported to me had the skills and knowledge to do well at their jobs, but they didn't take the work seriously enough to excel. That put a cap on how well we could perform as a team.

There's a lot of talk out there about how to motivate people, and some of it's good, but when it comes down to it, as a leader, you can only provide the fuel. It's up to the individual to provide the match. A good motivational talk can get you excited, but when it comes to actually doing the work, you've got to light your own fire. I knew I couldn't make my staff be more motivated, just as I couldn't instill desire or pride in them. With that in mind, I let three of the managers go and expanded the territory of the fourth. I took the rest of the region for myself. From then on, it would be down to just the two of us, but it was a team I felt I could win with.

Every week, from Monday through Friday, I was on the road, working my accounts. It wasn't easy, but it was the right thing to do. From my days in the NFL, I'd learned how to maximize my travel schedule, so within that time, I was able to cover a lot of ground. My colleague similarly held up her end, and after just eight months, the numbers reflected our work. We showed an increase in not only profitability but also market share, and once again, my efforts were duly acknowledged.

After two years at Schreiber, I was relocated back to Green Bay. I was to lead a team that would manage the largest food distributor group in the US, with forty-five operating companies. As part of my strategy, instead of having company reps divided by geographic region, I decided to shift to organization-specific sales reps. This approach ended up being so successful that Schreiber adopted it throughout the company.

So far, I was able to do exactly what I'd wanted. Thanks to a steep learning curve, I'd been able to fill the gaps in my resume. I gained invaluable experience in logistics, inventory management, quality control, production, and research and development. After three and a half years, I felt I was ready for the next step. As it happened, a once-in-a-lifetime chance was about to materialize.

For more than thirty-five years, Schreiber had been a major supplier of cheese for McDonald's. During this entire time, the account had been managed exclusively by one person, and he was about to retire. Not only was McDonald's our biggest and most important customer, it was also the most visible. It was the only customer for whom the CEO followed daily reports. As went McDonald's, so went Schreiber.

As expected, the job opening drew the attention of candidates from every department throughout the company, including me. My competition included management-level staff from sales, finance, operations, quality assurance, production, and inventory management. Because the position required expertise in all these areas, it was anyone's ball game.

After a series of initial interviews, the search team narrowed the pool to three, of which I was one. The other two candidates each had more than twenty years of experience with Schreiber. On paper, their qualifications far exceeded mine, but if a winning team was selected based only on their stats, there'd be no reason to play the game. As long as I was in the race, there was still a chance.

The decision would be made by three board members, one of whom was the CEO. They would make their selection based heavily on personal interviews with each of us. This was the magic moment—the championship game.

When I sat for my interview, they asked basically one question: What quality do you think is most important in the management of McDonald's? As far as I was concerned, they'd put their pitch right over the plate, so without hesitation, I took a huge swing.

"Trust," I said immediately.

"Why is that?" one board member asked.

"Trust is the foundational element upon which all relationships are built," I said, then illustrated it with a variety of experiences in which I'd seen that to be true.

"And how do you build trust?" another questioned.

"Speak from the heart. Be consistent. Follow through on your commitments at every level of service and in every interaction. Be accountable. Show empathy, in all things, at all times." I said, "At the most basic level, whether you're running the company or working in the plant, we're all just people trying to navigate the unexpected and uncharted, hoping to reach a mutually beneficial goal. The way I see it, *You Win with People* isn't just a book title; it's a formula for success."

Apparently, the committee agreed, because I was named the next director of the McDonald's business unit. I don't know how much their decision hinged on the interview versus my past performance, but what it boiled down to was trust. Not only because that was my response to them, but because the board members trusted *me*. They knew that no matter who I was meeting with, in every situation, I knew how to handle myself and would represent the company well. I was a people person, and my beliefs and values were unquestionable. They also trusted that I would leave no doubt in my performance, and knew that the same trust and faith would be shared by McDonald's.

My first introduction to McDonald's happened when my boss, the senior vice president of food service, took me to meet with the McDonald's senior vice president of purchasing. After introductions and some small talk, the McDonald's VP looked to my boss. "Does he have the authority and responsibility to make decisions on behalf of Schreiber Foods?" he asked.

"He does."

With that, the McDonald's executive rose from his chair and shook my hand. "If you ever need anything, you come and see me," he said. With that, the meeting was over. Done deal. That interaction and handshake told me all I needed to know about what trust meant to McDonald's.

As I later learned, that handshake was more than a gesture—it represented how our two companies did business. Over the life of the partnership, there had never been a formal contract or agreement binding the organizations. The terms were mutually assured by an unspoken promise. I wouldn't have to build trust with McDonald's; rather, I would have to ensure I didn't do anything to disrupt the faith and confidence the companies already had in one another.

I had much to learn about McDonald's, but when it came to leadership, it was largely plug and play. As always, I relied on the basics—the fundamentals. One of those fundamentals was communication.

As I knew, when making good decisions, information is king. That was never truer than at McDonald's. With such a big account and so many moving parts, often much of the information I needed to manage their business was spread out among multiple teams, each working on different aspects of the same projects. Much to my chagrin, these teams often made decisions that I wouldn't find out about until later. Sometimes much later. For me to do my job effectively, I needed to get that information sooner. The earlier I received it, the more time I had to react.

Coaches who are successful and who are in the game for the long haul aren't successful because they're geniuses in certain realms. It's because they possess an ability to communicate. If you can't connect with your people, you might as well find another line of work.

I carried coaching into leadership, because that's what I knew. Most people get these skills from a speaker or a book or a class. I'm always suspicious of leaders who learned entirely through classroom theory and not on the ground. Many of the people who teach leadership in universities have never been in the work world outside of academia.

I've found that if someone is successful, yet their lived background doesn't contribute to where they are, their skills probably came naturally. In other words, there was some amount of luck involved. Their abilities weren't earned and learned through hard work and trial and error. There's a value to God-given talent, to be sure. Some truly great players operate on instinct, yet they can't tell you how they got there. They have no idea. To me, the best coaches and leaders are the ones who had to really work at it. To develop. Those are the folks you really want to look to for learning.

People like Bill Gates and Steve Jobs are really popular in some circles, but to me, they're the people I least want to try to emulate. My worldview is so totally different from theirs that I question what I could learn from them. What I really admire about people like Charlie Munger and Warren Buffett is that those guys aren't only smart, they also frame their intellect in terms of common sense. To me, that's wisdom—people who can package their smarts and their experience in a way that others can understand. You can have all the knowledge or know-how in the world, but if you can't communicate it, it's essentially useless for building and leading successful teams.

When it came to my own team and getting the information I needed in a more timely manner, I could have instituted a formal system of communication, but I opted for a more personal approach. I found that the most current and accurate information came from direct, impromptu conversations with people on the ground—people who had critical knowledge about projects that impacted Schreiber's business with McDonald's. That was true on both sides of the account. I needed to know what was going on at Schreiber, but I also needed insight into the workings at McDonald's. For that, I needed proximity.

I leased an apartment that I also used as my off-site office in Oak Brook, Illinois, near the McDonald's headquarters. Then, it was back on the road. For the next three years, every Monday, I made the four-hour drive from Green Bay to Oak Brook, returning home on Friday.

My strategy paid off sooner than expected. Four months into my new schedule, during which I spent as much time as possible asking questions and listening intently to the answers, I got a critical piece of information. During a watercooler conversation, someone in new-product development told me that McDonald's was preparing to launch a new sandwich nationally. I hadn't known, because the cheese for the new sandwich was one they were already using in other products. However, there was one ingredient that did interest me— precooked bacon.

A few years earlier, as part of its efforts to diversify our product line, Schreiber had purchased a precooked bacon company. The plant was located about a hundred miles from my Oak Brook office. I told this to my buyer at McDonald's and naively assumed that he would just accept us as one of their suppliers. What I didn't know was that he already had three other suppliers in the system and didn't need a fourth. In addition, there was an extensive and very specific protocol through which new products were approved. The process for Schreiber's product to get accepted could take a year or more, and the launch was scheduled to start in just three months.

I had no idea how to pull it off, but I knew I didn't want to let the opportunity pass us by. In the end, I might not be successful, but if I at least tried, I knew I'd learn some invaluable information. The way I saw it, it was all upside. So I went for it.

I started by obtaining a sample of the bacon McDonald's had approved for the new sandwich. I drove it to our bacon plant, and within three days, they had a prototype that was similar to the target sample. I brought it to McDonald's. It would take three more prototypes, but eventually our product was accepted as a match. That was one hurdle, but the fact remained that McDonald's didn't need another supplier.

A few weeks later, I was headed home when I got a call from my buyer. "Do you hear that sound?" he said. "That's the sound of someone knocking on the door of opportunity."

As it happened, one of the other suppliers had experienced a production breakdown. The upshot was that they would only be able to fulfill 70 percent of their committed volume. Since we already had an approved product, Schreiber was in a position to walk right through that door. With that, we became a bacon supplier to McDonald's. Not only did we gain market share, but I also netted huge gains in the categories of goodwill, trust, and value. It strengthened our partnership with McDonald's and, as a result, was a catalyst to my career. And it all started with a commitment to communication, and more specifically to listening.

Not long ago, I came across an article in *The New York Times* by Aneesh Raman and Maria Flynn. The pair explained why, in the age of advanced computing and AI, human skills—especially so-called soft skills—will matter more than ever. The article quoted Minouche Shafik, the president of Columbia University at the time, who said, "In the past, jobs were about muscles. Now they're about brains, but in the future, they'll be about the heart." I think of communication as part of that heart.

So often, when I look around organizations, especially at the leadership level, I see an inability to communicate married to an inability to listen. When those leaders talk about "soft skills," it's often derisive—I think because they know they don't have them. But humans will always be fundamentally human. Connecting at the level of our shared humanity is both the most meaningful and the most effective thing we can do. It's good for the bottom line any way you slice it. When people want to feel more connected to their work, it's rarely about the actual skills they're employing. They want to feel more connected as a human being. Providing that connection produces dividends all the way around—your team will be more satisfied and more dedicated. And it comes down to making and nurturing real relationships.

All that said, not every aspect of leadership came naturally to me, given my coaching experience. During a 360 review with my team, one thing that came out loud and clear was that

I was too negative. That's how I was perceived. It turned out that my relentless focus on pointing out what could be improved was a little too much for my staff, who viewed it more as constant criticism. I was guilty as charged. Yet there was more to the story, as I explained to them.

"What you don't know is the spirit in which my observations are being delivered," I said. "In sports, you spend all your time looking for areas that need to be improved. The best teams are the ones that pay attention to those details. That delve down to the level of the micro. Any coach at the top of their game is able to analyze their team that way, and any player at the top of their game is able to analyze themselves in that same way. The problem is, that's not common. Everyone wants to watch the tackle they made ten times over, but they want to fast-forward through their mistakes. It's up to the coach to identify things the players either can't see or don't want to see." I explained that my job as a leader was to make them more successful, and for that to happen, they had to improve.

Yet in my zeal to be a great coach, I'd forgotten that my team members were not athletes. They hadn't grown up in the environment I had. When you grow up playing sports, if you have solid coaches, you get used to hearing more criticism than accolades.

Once my team understood where I was coming from and my motivation, they accepted my insights more willingly. I don't know that they ever liked it, but they saw the rationale behind it, and they got tougher skin. I also met them in the middle. I wasn't as negative as I had been and became less stingy with validation. We found a happy medium. And I believe that ethos of welcoming feedback started to permeate the company.

It's a rare soul who is born loving feedback. Perhaps there's no such person. When my oldest son, Tyler, came to Green

Bay, he was ten years old. I believed he needed to do something he was responsible for, so he decided to take a paper route. He was diligent. He learned the route and was reliable, making his deliveries like clockwork to forty or fifty households. The problem was, he wouldn't collect money. He was afraid his customers might give him some kind of negative feedback.

I told him feedback wasn't something to be afraid of. For instance, if we go to a restaurant and something isn't quite right, the people who work there won't know unless we tell them. Otherwise, they'll keep doing it, and they could lose our business. So, chances are they'd rather know so that we'll come back. When it comes down to it, you're only as good as the feedback you receive. If you get positive feedback, you'll keep doing it. If you get negative feedback, you can change it. So giving someone feedback is a favor. And when you give it, you want to frame it as a positive, to help that person be successful.

For about six months, I floated the money Tyler had to pay to procure the newspapers, but then I drew the line. I told him, "Look, these people order the paper expecting to pay, and they expect you to be the one to collect." The first time he did it, I went with him. He was so embarrassed to knock on the door and ask for money. But after a time, he realized that feedback comes in many forms. Sometimes, when he collected payment, he'd also get tips—maybe at Christmas, in bad weather, and so on.

When it comes to your employees, even though they aren't your customers, their satisfaction is important. That means giving them clear, open, and honest communication so they can know where they stand at all times. Sometimes, it's the uncertainty that's the worst thing.

Woody once said, "When I walk into a room, I want to be able to separate people by putting the people who hate me on one side of the room and the people who love me on the other. I respect each of them equally. It's the sons of bitches in the middle I don't like. I don't trust them, because I don't know where they stand."

In time, I was promoted once again. After one year of managing the McDonald's account, I became the vice president of the McDonald's business unit and an officer at Schreiber Foods. It was a proud day, to be sure. However, midway through my career there, I hit a roadblock that could have derailed everything.

A client of Eileen's was purchased by a Fortune 500 company, and the CEO asked her to join his staff as the vice president of marketing, managing a department of about 140 employees. The problem was that their headquarters was in Louisville, Kentucky. Eileen had followed me and supported my career ever since we were married. Though she kept working, she'd largely occupied positions for which she was overqualified and that lacked challenge, excitement, and leadership opportunities. It was time for me to do my part to support her career.

McDonald's didn't care where I lived, because they knew they could depend on me regardless. It was Schreiber's reaction I was concerned about. The company valued officers being involved in the community, as well as having a presence in the corporate office. I explained the situation to our CEO and told him I planned to relocate. "So why are we having this conversation?" he said. We agreed that I would spend one week per month at Schreiber's corporate headquarters, and that was that.

I was now supporting Schreiber's interests not only in Oak Brook but also in other parts of the US, Brazil, Mexico, and Europe. Between that and my time in Green Bay, I was traveling almost nonstop. Eileen was thoroughly immersed in her new position and the boys in their lives, so I had a lot of latitude and flexibility in meeting my responsibilities at home. For her part, Eileen actually enjoyed it, because the separations made it feel to her like we were dating again. For my part, I enjoyed the fact that being home only occasionally meant I was seldom in trouble.

We rolled along in this way for eight years, before an incident none of us could have foreseen changed our lives indelibly.

Eileen had been working as part of a team that was about to launch a new product for Wall Street. She, along with other members of the company's senior leadership, traveled to New York for the presentation. The evening before, the group dined at Windows on the World. It was September 10, 2001.

The next morning, the group was loading their luggage into their vans to travel several blocks to the meeting site. Just then, the first plane crashed into the World Trade Center. Eileen was standing next to the van and saw it happen.

What followed was nothing short of a nightmare. Thanks to some creative problem-solving and the help of a bus driver who turned out to be more of a guardian angel, Eileen and her team arrived safely back in Louisville the next morning. I was on the road to Green Bay at the time and didn't hear about the event until well after it had happened. When I got word, I immediately took the next off-ramp and headed back to Louisville.

The attacks had a lasting impact on most Americans, but even more so on those who were at ground zero. Eileen struggled to deal with what she'd experienced, and though therapy helped, over time, she knew that something in her would never be the same. Her outlook on life had shifted. While she valued her work, she decided that she needed to be of more direct service to others. It was time to give back. The following year, she retired and turned her considerable energies toward pro bono and nonprofit work.

My younger son, Brady, had been knocking around, trying

to find his place in the world. He decided to enlist in the army and was assigned to the 101st Airborne. By 9/11, he'd been on active duty for three years, including sixteen months in Kosovo. After the attack, he was among the first troops deployed to Kandahar, Afghanistan. He served for a total of seven years and was discharged as a sergeant. From there, he became a police officer in Wisconsin.

As for me, the new travel restrictions made a lifestyle that was already getting old start to feel close to unbearable. My knees weren't enjoying it either. After I left the NFL, I'd had multiple knee surgeries to try to correct some of the damage done by decades of football, but they were no longer up to the task of incessant travel. In 2004, I had a bilateral knee replacement, which made for a commotion going through airport security.

One day in 2009, as I pulled into an airport parking lot, I simply couldn't will myself to get out of the car. I had reached my end. I couldn't endure one more metal detector, pat down, baggage search, flight cancellation, rental car, or hotel room. I was on the road so much that more than once, I forgot what city I was in, what hotel I was staying at, or which rental car was mine. With that, I put the car in gear and drove the sixteen hours to my destination.

Shortly after that, I tendered my resignation. I told my CEO that I was not retiring from the job but from the travel. It came as a surprise to most of my colleagues. I was the guy who got there first in the morning, ate lunch at my desk, and was the last to leave. I wasn't so much a workaholic as a perfectionist. I was never *the* best at anything, but no one ever worked harder to be *their* best. For me, that was success.

Many doubted whether I was capable of retiring. And why would I? I was only sixty years old, in good health, and making a valuable contribution to the company. But the way I viewed it, I wasn't so much retiring as I was refocusing. I would simply apply my passion, energy, and drive to helping others find their success. The only question was: Where?

Eileen and I had enjoyed the fourteen years we'd lived in Louisville, but because of our schedules, with few exceptions, we hadn't had the time to develop the kinds of close friendships I'd had in Cleveland and Green Bay. We decided to go somewhere neither of us had ever lived before. The location needed to be a day's drive to our families in northeast Ohio, to have moderate weather with all four seasons, and to be small enough to make daily life a no-hassle experience yet large enough to offer good health care, a diverse demographic, and great restaurants.

A friend suggested we explore Asheville, North Carolina. We knew nothing about the town, but after several visits, we were in love. Asheville had an energy and a vibe that was contagious. It seemed like everyone you met was in a good mood. The way I calculated it, the town comprised four main groups: lifelong residents whose families had been there for generations, people with a passion for the outdoors and the mountains, those who chose to retire there because of the climate and way of life, and tourists—more than twelve million annually at that time. The average age in Asheville was just thirty-seven. To me, the best way to stay young was to be around young people. It's like catching a cold—you hang around someone who has one.

And so Asheville it was. We sold our place in Louisville, packed our bags, and prepared for the next phase of life.

Part Three

CHAPTER 15

Failing at Retirement

I didn't have a plan for my retirement, but that didn't concern me. I had total confidence that I'd figure it out. I set out on what seemed like a logical path, essentially walking in Eileen's footsteps by seeking ways to give back. Certainly, there would be organizations that would benefit from the knowledge and experience I had to offer, younger people who needed mentoring, and golf balls that needed whacking. Okay, so golf wasn't exactly community service, but it was on my radar as an area where I could focus some of my newly available energy and attention. I'd always enjoyed playing but, due to my work schedule, had only ever been able to get out on the occasional Saturday. Now that I had more time, I considered turning my hobby into a serious pursuit.

For starters, though, we needed a place to live. Eileen and I hired an architect to begin sketching out our dream home. Over the years, we'd amassed a collection of all the features and elements we liked in a house, with the intention of one day applying them to a creation of our own. But planning quickly became unwieldy, and we realized we'd do much better managing a renovation than a new build. Plus, the stakes with a renovation were lower—there was less risk involved in redesigning a proven structure than constructing a new one. Now to find the house.

Rather than hire a Realtor, we prevailed upon some friends to show us around various Asheville neighborhoods. We ended up driving past a house in their neighborhood with a "For Sale" sign out front. But while the sign was visible, little about the house was. I had to walk all the way down the driveway to even see it, because the mass of vegetation out front was so dense it obstructed any real view of the structure.

Once I was able to see past the jungle that was the yard, my interest was piqued. The home was at an interesting and unique elevation, and it had some eye-catching elements. The sleigh roofline, the eyebrow-style dormer windows, the incorporation of copper, and the overall detailing set it apart from the other houses we'd seen. The wood shake siding gave it an appearance of a home you might find on Cape Cod, yet it didn't look out of place in the densely forested landscape of Asheville.

With the help of a Realtor, we were able to schedule a showing for the next day. It was the same principle as when I'd met Eileen and knew almost instantly that she was perfect for me. Within just thirty minutes, we were ready to make an offer. I had no problem making quick decisions if I knew what I was trying to achieve. I had learned that lesson negotiating player contracts. Going in, I knew what I wanted and what I was willing to concede (and of course, Eileen had her say as well), so the process went quickly. We closed on the house in December 2009, a week after making our offer.

Eileen had a friend in Louisville who was an interior designer, and between the two of them, they led the renovation of our new home. The house was one story with no hallways and ten-foot ceilings. The exterior was designed to suggest a second level, but really it was akin to a 1970s-style ranch. We ended up making no structural changes, but the interior was fully recast. A chef's kitchen with new appliances and countertops, new fireplace facing and light fixtures, French doors, wall coverings, drapes, vanities, carpeting, bathroom fixtures . . . And while we didn't change the bones of the house, we did change the appearance of the structure by adding a beam system in the family room, along with a cathedral ceiling. That fall, just as the leaves were changing on the thousands of trees in our new neighborhood, the renovation was complete. The results were stunning. There was no doubt about it—we were home.

The outside, however, was another story.

The only experience I'd had with yards had been limited to cutting grass, along with some minor landscaping projects I'd done while working odd jobs in Cleveland. Our new home had foliage so dense you could barely get around the yard. The ground had an interesting slope—a contour that was rolling and slightly hilly, with a tall embankment between our property and the road. I liked the property's geography, but the present landscaping failed to capitalize on the unique opportunities—or to take into account the special challenges— it provided.

The first order of business would be to thin things out. The vegetation was so thick and unwieldy that I knew the clearing process would be slow, tedious, and accompanied by no shortage of colorful language. Not an appealing prospect.

By that time, it was February, and though the winters don't get especially cold in Asheville—maybe cold by San Francisco standards, but certainly not if you've lived in Green Bay—it was chilly enough. I declared that daytime highs in the upper forties were too cold for outdoor work and kicked that particular can down the road for at least a few months. Instead, I focused on how I might engage with my new community.

In short order, we met several people who were well connected within Asheville's business community, as well as some of the broader initiatives that were happening within the town. Eileen had completed a program called Leadership Asheville, which was designed to educate new residents about various projects and opportunities, along with the local chamber of commerce and board of tourism. From that experience, she'd developed some good contacts and introduced me to a few of them.

As word about me—my prior experience and the fact that I was interested in getting involved—got out, I was invited to join several boards. In the end, I accepted invitations to become a mentor in an entrepreneurial program sponsored by Leadership Asheville, and agreed to join two boards.

As it happened, one of the premier private golf clubs in the country was located about a mile from our new home. The course was built in 1923 on land that had once belonged to the Vanderbilt estate. One thing I had not been ready to retire from was competition, along with the relentless pursuit of improvement. Those genes were still very much alive in me, so I joined the club with the aim of improving my game to a level where I could be competitive in local and regional senior tournaments.

When you retire, you don't give up your DNA. The things that make you who you are are still there. What changes is what you apply those inner workings to. It's a matter of refocusing. Now it seemed my refocus plan was gaining some clarity.

I attacked each new initiative with the same dedication, commitment, and energy as I had my work life and pretty much everything else I'd ever taken on. I always had a plan, I prepared, and I did my best. I followed this system vigorously and faithfully for about two years before I realized that all my hard work and dedication simply wasn't bearing fruit.

For the most part, Asheville didn't have the type of big corporations or organizations I was accustomed to working with. Most of the business-oriented folks were entrepreneurs launching small startups. They—both the ventures and the people behind them—were another beast entirely from what I was accustomed to. As a result, they didn't want my knowledge in sales, leadership, people development, or motivation. They certainly weren't interested in hearing advice or insights from someone older than their parents.

In life, it doesn't matter what you're good at, it's whether someone needs or wants it. Regardless of how successful you were in your profession, the question is how relevant that profession and those skills are to the people you're trying to connect with. If there's a mismatch, it's game over. It seemed like no one wanted what I had to offer. It felt as if overnight my hard-won career skills simply became irrelevant.

My experiences on the boards I'd joined were equally unsuccessful. As I discovered, most of the other members were there because of the status it brought them. Others just wanted the opportunity to spout their opinions and weren't particularly interested in meaningful involvement. The result was a lot of talk with few results. Not the place for me. They, however, thought the boards were working just fine. With no indication that the situation would improve, I resigned. That left golf.

I'd remained consistent in my attempts to develop my golf game, committing to weekly lessons. Parts of my swing were good, but others needed to be fixed. The problem was that I didn't know which was which. Continuing the same habits made me consistent, but not better. To improve, I needed a coach who could recognize my strengths—even when they were inconsistent with what were considered "proper" methods—and correct what needed correcting.

I loved golf—the fact that it was an individual sport, got me outdoors, and provided an opportunity to apply myself to a pursuit where I might improve. Yet as time went on, I realized that perhaps one of the reasons I'd liked golf so much during my work years was because my access to it had been limited. The restriction made it that much sweeter when I finally got to play. Now that I could play all the time, the game lost some of its allure, yet I was still committed to becoming a better player.

What was most important to me wasn't just getting out there—I didn't play for the love of the game. I played with a goal of becoming good enough to hold my own at any level. I needed to be in the high single digits on a consistent basis. To improve to that degree, I had to focus on the intricacies of my swing, but I couldn't find a teacher who could get me there.

Each of the instructors I worked with had their own way of teaching—their own rigid opinion of what the "right" swing should be and how to achieve it. Yet if you look at the best players today, many have techniques that aren't at all classic. They're able to compete at the top because they're working with an instructor who understands how to preserve their natural strengths and build a custom game around them. It was the same with great football coaches. We all knew the "proper" stance, but if you had a guy with a jacked-up stance who performed consistently at a high level, you didn't touch it. You worked with it.

Every instructor I encountered was convinced they knew what was right and what was wrong, and each tried to make me fit into their mold. They had me change things about my game that had actually been working for me, and so should have been left as is. But they didn't know how to work that way.

As a result, the more I played, the worse I got, which defeated all my intentions.

Among sailors, there's a saying that the two best days of a boat owner's life are the day they buy the boat and the day they sell it. When you arrive at the point when leaving something feels better than staying, you know it's time to go. That became my sentiment about golf. One day, I walked off the course, put my bag in the garage, and said, "I'm done." I haven't touched a set of clubs since, and that was five years ago as of this writing.

My first efforts at retirement had left me discouraged and disillusioned. It was time for plan B. I would try to help the community in my own way.

Growing up, I was no stranger to poverty. If you had a poured foundation under your trailer rather than cinder blocks, you were better off than most. All around me was a mini version of *Hillbilly Elegy*, an economic and emotional landscape that included inadequate housing, hunger, and lack of medical care, all of which led to depression, despair, and addiction.

Though Asheville was a far cry from my hometown in Ohio, it had its own share of problems relative to homelessness and economic insecurity. There were a variety of nonprofits whose mission was to solve these problems, but rather than only donating money to them as we had been, I decided to go one step further. I would take the problem on myself.

I was aware of two families in need of help. Both had many challenges that stemmed largely from housing insecurity. One comprised a single mother in her mid-thirties with a thirteen-year-old daughter. They moved frequently, living wherever they could find shelter. When I met them, they were temporarily set up in a run-down, overcrowded trailer with friends.

The mother had become addicted to drugs in her mid-teens. Eventually, she was incarcerated. In her twenties, she successfully completed a court-ordered drug-treatment plan and had remained drug-free ever since. Having seen up close the devastating effects of drug abuse, especially on children, I felt for her, and I knew it was no small thing that she had been able to stay clean.

The other family was a married couple with four children between the ages of three and nine. The husband had been medically discharged from the armed forces and suffered with PTSD. At the time I met them, they were staying in cramped quarters with her parents.

After some research, I located a quarter-acre lot with two new trailers adjacent to each other. They were identical units, twelve hundred square feet with three bedrooms and two full baths. I purchased both units and installed all new appliances. I also built a six-foot wooden fence around the property, then sodded the yard so the children would have a nice place to play. To add to the curb appeal, I created a raised stone flower bed around the front entrance of each unit and planted shrubs and perennials. By the time I was done, both units were turnkey.

The plan was to offer the families flexible lease payments. They would pay for their own utilities, then beyond that, whatever they could afford for rent.

For the mother and daughter, that initially amounted to zero. The mother was starting a new job and was carrying debt that she was trying to pay off. I knew up front that she would be unable to pay any rent for a period of time, and that was okay.

The second family qualified for federal housing assistance. The first year, that paid for 90 percent of the rent for which the property qualified, leaving the tenants to pay the remaining 10 percent plus utilities. Each year, the program would pay 10 percent less, and the tenants would make up the gap.

Two years passed, and in the end, I didn't renew either lease. The single mother not only never contributed to the rent but also failed to pay her utilities. In the second year, the family of six never paid their share of the rent. Yet my decision wasn't really based on finances. I could have accepted their delinquencies if it hadn't been for their attitudes.

From the day both families moved in, there was friction between them. I routinely received calls and texts from each of them complaining about the other. I'd signed on to be a landlord and property manager, but now I was also a counselor. Perhaps that would have been all right here and there, but it was evident that neither family was invested in doing their own work. There was no sense of accountability or personal responsibility. Instead, it was all a game of finger-pointing.

The irony was that both families were alike. They felt entitled, were devoid of pride, and blamed their circumstances entirely on others. Yet when people did try to assist them, they had little to no appreciation for those efforts.

Once again, I'd failed. The way I saw it afterward, the problem was my own unrealistic expectations. I thought the help I was providing would be enough to change something for these families—to give them at least enough hope, encouragement, and motivation that they could build on it.

Instead, they continued the patterns they'd lived with for probably their entire lives. They had not struggled enough yet to commit to a change. When I met them, they were on their way to rock bottom, but they hadn't yet reached it. It seemed they'd have to get all the way there before they were willing to meet an opportunity halfway, investing their own energy in shifting their circumstances. As it was, they didn't yet have the incentive to change.

I know shifting your mindset is no small feat. But I also know that when it comes down to it, real change is an inside job. As I'd learned from decades of coaching and being coached—but had forgotten in my zeal to try to make a real difference in someone's life—someone outside you can't actually motivate you. The most they can do is light the fire, but you have to build it. These folks didn't have the kindling, and that wasn't something I could provide for them.

All my suppositions were confirmed after they vacated the property and I went to inspect what was left. It was nothing but squalor, damage, and destruction—I imagine perhaps an outward manifestation of how they felt inside. Both units had been gutted to the studs. They'd taken the appliances, fixtures, doors, flooring—everything. I told them both that I hoped they never realized the opportunity they'd squandered; otherwise, they might never forgive themselves.

In life, some people are ready for help, whether it's help escaping poverty, help developing their career or a new skill set, or so on. With these folks, your time and energy are a worthwhile investment. But sadly, I think that's a relatively small percentage of the population. When people aren't there—when they aren't ready to meet your energy with their own—it's effort wasted. That's why when nonprofits ask would-be donors for money, those donors often want to see that the nonprofit has first been able to do something for themselves in the way of fundraising. They want to see a workable plan and real commitment. Otherwise, whatever money they get is likely to go to waste. It's wonderful to want to help people, but as was sadly underscored for me by this incident, there's little you can do if they don't want to help themselves.

After nearly three years, all my well-intended efforts had come to naught. In life, you don't want to force yourself to keep doing something that doesn't make you happy and where you're not making a real difference for the people you're doing it for. That's a bad formula not only for retirement but for any kind of experience. That described everything I'd pursued up to that point. It was time to make another shift, but in what direction?

Around the time I quit golf, I was introduced to three

young men in their thirties. I'd been recommended to them as someone who might help them with their startup. They wanted to develop an app that could be used by youth soccer teams. In their vision, the app would provide a mechanism through which parents, coaches, and related organizations could communicate privately. It would also include features to improve the players' training and conditioning.

The founders had formed a company six months prior to our meeting. They'd hired an outside firm to build the app, which was estimated to take about a year. Beyond that, they had nothing—no money, no office, and no plan. Just the idea. That's why they came to me.

At first glance, the situation reminded me of when I'd joined the Invaders. The owner had a franchise, but no real understanding of what needed to be done to field a team or play a game. The only difference was that the owner had some sense of what he was doing, whereas these guys didn't. The bigger problem was, neither did I.

I decided to throw in my lot with these guys, and I did it for all the wrong reasons. I was bored. I thought too highly of my own abilities. And I placed faith in people I should not have. But I mean, other than that, what could go wrong? It would not take long to find out. I was to quickly learn what happened when I violated every instinct and principle I had, all in the name of pride, legacy, and ego.

The success of the venture relied on technology. The problem was that there was nothing proprietary, new, or innovative about the concept. For my part, I knew nothing about technology or what went into building an app. That was my first mistake—I was out of my area.

My second mistake was that, having found myself out of my area, I should have hired a chief technology officer to manage the firm that was building the app. I didn't have the knowledge required to know what they should be doing and to hold them accountable. As it was, the contractor was dishonest about their capabilities and their commitment. They were not engaged or qualified enough to deliver on their commitments, and on our side, we had no one who could recognize that and call "Bullshit!" By all accounts, it was a complete disaster.

The result was the loss of two and a half years of effort, several hundred thousand dollars of my own investment, and an app that was never launched. Simply put, it was the biggest embarrassment of my life.

The startup was officially the worst decision I had ever made. I violated every principle of engaging in something new, and I paid a steep price for it—financially, emotionally, and psychologically. To this day, I can't think of one thing we did right, except throwing in the towel and closing the doors with no debt.

At this point, the startup was the icing on a very bitter cake. I was confronted with the fact that I hadn't just been un-successful at launching an app and I hadn't simply made a bad investment. At that moment, I was faced with one larger, com-pletely inescapable fact: Any way you sliced it, my retirement had been an absolute failure.

In retrospect, which is where pretty much all wisdom is ac-quired, I understand that you can't truly anticipate what life will be like postwork until you're actually retired. When we contemplate retirement, we tend not to think so much about what we're moving into but what we're moving away from. On not having to work anymore (or for me, not having to travel). We're happy that we no longer have to do all the things we disliked about work.

We tend to picture retirement as being like when a spouse goes out of town for a few days. Suddenly, you're flush with freedom, realizing you can do whatever you want, including things you don't normally feel the autonomy to do. You have no responsibilities. The world is your oyster! Yet the reality is that after a relatively short period of time, when you've been there and done that, you suddenly realize that you don't know what to do next. You miss the structure and familiarity of everyday life.

You imagine there's going to be so much euphoria when you retire, and there is, but it wears off. Without a job, there's no real distinction between weekdays and weekends. Psychologically and emotionally, it's surprisingly difficult to come to terms with the fact that you have total access to your time.

It seems that the solution, then, is to devise a plan for retirement in advance. But while it's good to have a plan for retirement, I think that as committed as you are to mapping out your future, you have to be equally committed to being flexible. The fact is that your plan either isn't going to work or will somehow be different than you envisioned. Even Eileen, whose plan to dive into nonprofit work went mostly as she envisioned, admits to having struggled to adjust to life postcareer.

For most, your plan won't be what you initially thought it was going to be, so arriving at a place that's fulfilling and enjoyable will require a lot of trial and error. That's not a bad thing; it's just challenging if you don't anticipate it. If, instead, you have a vision of perfection. In other words, if you approach retirement like I did. In reality, retiring—like pretty much anything else in life that's worth doing—takes practice.

Going from an entire day of structure to an entire day lacking structure will require you to fill in your own blanks. You can find a pattern and simply put it on repeat, like the guys I know who golf every day, but for me—and I bet for most people, perhaps including them—that won't provide a sense of meaning or satisfaction.

A mistake we make is that we focus on the practicalities, on how we'll fill our schedule. But it's not necessarily about what you *do* in retirement, but what you want to *get out* of retirement that you need to identify. For instance, I focused on the idea that I could suddenly work out whenever I wanted to, but that quickly lost its shine. Big deal. Then, I realized where the real opportunity was—to enhance my health. That was important to me. Working out was something I was doing, but better health was something I was gaining.

With golf, I thought I wanted to achieve some level of competitiveness. That was my target. Looking back, what I really wanted was to achieve something worthy of recognition. Mentoring, meanwhile, was about the opportunity to give back.

You might decide that when you retire, you want to learn a foreign language. I promise you that you'll abandon your lessons unless you have a larger goal. Maybe you want to expand your world by traveling to France or to Italy—that's a different motivation. Or perhaps you want to develop richer relationships with your family, and so you decide to spend more time with your grandchildren. When you've identified the larger gain—something more than an arbitrary goal—then you can think about what steps you can take to get there.

I can see all of that clearly now, but at the time, I was mired in a fog of despair. Every swing I'd taken was a miss. I'd struck out, and was unsure what to do next. Here I was, this supposedly successful person who was in the prime of my retirement, and I'd never felt so lost.

Without somewhere to apply myself, every day began to mirror the one before. I had nothing that motivated me. I began to wake up in a bad mood, with nothing I could think of that would get me excited about the day. There was nothing I wanted to do or be a part of. When I looked around, what I saw inside others was a reflection of my own bleak mood. I couldn't find any good in anyone, especially myself.

I began to take everything out on Eileen. I was reluctant

to engage in conversation or show any kind of emotion. The more I acted out, the worse I felt. I could see what I was doing to Eileen and others around me, but I didn't know what to do about it. I didn't know how to change, because I didn't know what was causing it—and you can't fix what you don't know. Needless to say, I was no fun to be around, and I knew it. People would invite us out, and I'd tell Eileen to just go without me.

I was aware of what was happening, but I didn't know why. I read books about depression and anxiety, but found no solutions. Eileen did everything she could think of to try and help, but she couldn't, really, because she didn't know what I was experiencing.

I became an almost total recluse. I didn't want to talk to anyone, go anywhere, or be with anyone. I'd spend my days trying to avoid any contact with others, including Eileen. I didn't want to subject anyone to my dark moods. I got to the point where I didn't even want to be in my own skin anymore. There was nothing in life that motivated me—nothing that engaged me. My fire had all but gone out.

Someone might have told me, "You just have to find something you're passionate about!" I've heard that one a lot, and it's common advice. People say the secret to living a good life or to being successful is to "find and follow your passion." Well, I don't believe that one bit. It's a fallacy. I know I'm in the minority in that opinion, but I believe this with all my heart. You might say I'm passionate about it!

There I was, having exhausted everything that in my prior life I was "passionate" about—at least by the classic definition of what people say "passion" is. What I discovered was that I wasn't actually passionate about any of it. Mentoring. Civic duty. Golf. Not only was I questioning what I was going to do, I also had nothing to guide me. My supposed passions had let me down.

I started questioning what passion actually was and what role it plays in our lives. I had a lot of questions but few answers, and I needed those answers before I could take another step. I didn't want to start doing something else just for the sake of it, only to be let down again. I needed direction.

As that year drew to a close, Eileen and I had a plan to meet some friends in Charleston, South Carolina, to spend New Year's Eve together. The day came when they were to arrive, and that morning, I decided to take a walk across Ravenel Bridge.

The iconic structure is two and a half miles long, connecting Mount Pleasant to Charleston. At its highest point, it sits 187 feet above the Cooper River. As I crossed the bridge, I made a point to stay away from the railing. I'd never been afraid of heights, but I was conscious of a need not to get too close to the edge. As I approached the apex of the bridge, my breathing suddenly accelerated, and my steps shortened. I'd never had a panic attack before, but I imagined I was at the beginning of one. I felt an urgent need to turn around. I never actually contemplated jumping, but something told me I had to get off the bridge as quickly as possible. That my life literally depended on it.

Back at the hotel, I told Eileen what had happened. She knew I must have been deeply shaken, because I rarely shared anything so vulnerable. Finally, I came clean. I told her that as hard as I tried, I could not overcome whatever was causing me to think and act the way I had been.

Unlike the families I had tried to help, I was all the way down—deeper than whale shit at the bottom of the ocean. The harshest of realities stared me in the face: There was a darkness inside me, and I had no idea where it came from. All my life, I'd been able to either outwork it or flat-out suppress it, but in the end, it had come for me. I didn't know what this thing inside me was; the only thing I did know was that if I wanted a life worth living, I would have to find out and deal with it. It was time to take off the mask. To discover who I truly was inside.

But to do that, I was going to have to do something I never would have imagined myself doing. To do something that seemed both foreign and terrifying to me, and that went against every emotional instinct I had. But the way I saw it, I was out of options.

I would have to seek professional help.

CHAPTER 16

Journey to Texas

Three weeks after that ominous bridge walk, I found myself sitting in an office at a highly regarded clinic in Texas, waiting to be admitted for a mental-health evaluation. In the past, I had never been worried, upset, or concerned when things were going badly, because I always knew why. It wasn't that things didn't bother me, but up to this point, I always knew the source of the problem, which meant I could figure out how to change it. When I was coaching the Invaders and we lost nine games in a row, I knew exactly why we were where we were and what we needed to do to fix it. From there, it was just inputs and outputs—keep doing the things you need to do to improve and wait for the inevitable shift.

For the first time in my life, I found myself in a situation where things were bad, and I didn't know why. The cause completely eluded me, and everything I'd tried to change the situation had failed. I was determined to find the *why*.

The way I see it, we spend 90 percent of our energy on finding the fix and very little trying to figure out why something broke in the first place. In reality, if you dedicate 90 percent of your energy to understanding the cause—to truly comprehending it on a very deep level—changing it becomes much easier, because you don't spend energy banging your head against a wall trying things that won't work.

As it was, things had become so backward in my mind that I couldn't see my own reality clearly. I knew that if I continued to live the way I was, I would continue to be miserable, and Eileen would be gone. For a split second, I actually thought that could be a net positive, because then I wouldn't have to worry about how my mood and behavior were affecting her. That was how skewed my thinking had become. Deep down, I knew I didn't actually want Eileen to leave me, and to keep that from happening, I had to take serious steps.

I'd held back from seeking traditional help for a few reasons. I didn't picture myself lying on a therapist's couch, spilling my guts week after week. I wasn't interested in regular sessions over a period of months or years. The slow-drip method was not for me. I was also aware of the many horror stories of patients getting poor treatment from supposedly skilled mental-health providers. I didn't want to spend my energy going from therapist to therapist, searching for one who seemed competent and like a good match for me.

Validation and a gentle pat on the back were not going to help me. I was ready to do the work, and I needed an intervention that could meet me where I was. To me, that looked like becoming a patient, and I was ready to admit myself anywhere and for however long it took to enact real change.

After my declaration that I needed help, I spent a week doing research, which included gathering recommendations from various specialists as well as my personal physician. In the end, I chose the clinic in Texas. In addition to the glowing reviews I'd read and heard, their approach was that they did not provide treatment until they knew precisely what they were treating. Everyone entering the clinic was given a rigorous evaluation that culminated in a diagnosis.

As I sat there, listening to the administrator explaining the clinic's practices, policies, and procedures, it was clear that I was no longer driving my own bus. It was like my freshman year of football all over again. I was expected to do what I was told, respect authority, and trust those in charge to help me. In a way, it was comforting, because it was familiar territory, the feeling that if I followed what I was told to do, however challenging it might be, I could expect a positive outcome.

All my belongings were secured in my personal locker and would stay there until my discharge. Included were my phone, wallet, watch, computer, and belt. My shaving kit and other toiletries were secured but made available for me to use in the mornings and evenings.

The room I was assigned had no lock on the door. There were no lamps with cords, and the mirror was made of polished metal instead of glass. There was nothing in the room or on my person that I could potentially use to cause myself harm. On top of that, throughout the night, staff conducted room checks every two hours.

The isolation and starkness of my new accommodations reminded me of the night we'd spent in the monastery before the Rose Bowl. Absent, of course, were the sugar cookies, apple, and hot chocolate at bedtime.

All the patients had access to a common lounge, which included a television and four computer terminals, so we were able to have contact with the outside world. Each person was also given a flip phone.

I was part of a group of twenty-four inpatients, twenty-two of whom were between the ages of nineteen and twenty-nine. One woman was in her forties, and then there was me, at age sixty-seven. Quickly, I acquired a rather predictable nickname: Gramps.

The schedule we were placed on was highly structured. Monday through Friday, we had breakfast at eight, lunch at noon, and dinner at five thirty. Lights out was at ten. Much of the day was spent in group therapy, in individual sessions with either my therapist or my social worker, or undergoing an assortment of tests. We had two sessions of group therapy each day, morning and afternoon. Over the course of four weeks, I learned a great deal about my cohort, but I learned even more about myself.

Many of the stories shared by others in the group coalesced around similar themes: drug and alcohol abuse growing up, parents who were not very involved in their lives, and attempts at suicide. It was apparent that most were in the program because they had no other choice—not in the same way that I had no other choice, but because they'd really run out of options. They'd been forced to be there either by their parents or the court system. As a result, most of them were not engaged in or committed to their own healing. They weren't in treatment to get help, but instead to avoid punishment.

As skilled as the clinic staff was, their ability to help me or anyone else was directly proportional to the effort we were willing to put into our own recovery. It came down to the information we were willing to share—to its depth, accuracy, and truthfulness. It was a "help me help you" situation.

I did my best to show up fully and to share whatever I could that might aid in my healing. My therapist said I was the ideal patient, because I was totally committed and there wasn't anywhere I was not willing to go. It was apparent that most of the others in my group did not share my frame of mind, but that was not my concern. I would have been happy for them to experience positive outcomes, but this was not a team sport. In the end, I think much of life is about the ways we can serve and assist others, but this was the rare exception. In this situation, the only person I was concerned with was myself. And of course I knew from my prior life experience that if an addict doesn't want assistance and isn't ready to change, there's nothing anyone else can do to help them.

My own struggle made me more understanding of what it's like to have a mental illness or an emotional breakdown. I am sympathetic to people who are in that situation especially because access to high-quality treatment is extremely limited. I was fortunate to have had the means to choose a clinic based on its quality of care rather than affordability.

As restricted as my freedoms were at the clinic, it felt like a relief—a healing of sorts. It was the same experience I'd had when I had bilateral knee replacement surgery. Following the surgery, I was administered pain medication, which is standard procedure for this type of surgery. Unfortunately, I don't tolerate the side effects associated with pain meds well. When it was time for my next injection, I refused. The nurse contacted my surgeon and informed him of my "irrational" decision, to which he replied, "If the dumb SOB doesn't want pain medication, don't give it to him." When I was being discharged three days later, my nurse asked me how I was able to tolerate the pain. I told her, the way I see it, there was good pain and bad pain. Bad pain was the feeling I'd had for the past five years. Every day, I knew the pain was going to get a little worse than the day before. Following my replacements, every day I would be getting better. That was good pain. That was the feeling I had at the clinic: Every day, I was getting better.

Finding solutions to problems is all about gathering information and data. I was discovering things about myself in therapy and group sessions, and the therapists were discovering things about me through testing and interviews. By the end of the four weeks, I had learned mental techniques that I could apply on my own to better manage my thoughts and emotions, but the most telling and valuable information came from my therapist's summary report.

Retirement has given me the chance to consider my life looking backward and forward. When I look backward, I see only missed opportunities, losses, and shortcomings. When I look forward, I see indecision and a vast unknown. Looking backward, I was a seeker—someone who rarely enjoyed the present, preferring instead to look for ways to achieve more, experience more, give more. Looking forward, there is nothing to set my sights on—no new challenges, exceeding expectations, or overachieving.

I believe this is why many successful people leave retirement and return to their work life. They realize you are either in the game or out of the game. Your successes are spoken of either in the past tense or present tense, and they prefer to be in the present.

At the clinic, I learned that, for me, having a goal and doing everything in my power to achieve it was like a drug. I was addicted to the success cycle, and probably always will be to some extent. The truth is, if I was back in the corporate world or on the football field, I would do it all over again. That's because the outcomes I was getting were feeding the addiction. It was a vicious cycle, but it did not feel like either—vicious or a cycle. I just thought, *Lucky me! I have the physiological intensity that allows me to perform at a high level. To succeed at most things I attempt.* When those internals meet an external culture that rewards that ethos, it's a dangerous mix.

I think anyone who excels at a high level, regardless of the area, has that same ability to push themselves past their limits, going places other people can't. But it's like alpine climbing: The best climbers are the ones who can push themselves to overcome extreme challenges, to suppress even their own need for oxygen to make the summit. Yet in the process, they may go so hard that they no longer have the reserves required to get safely back down the mountain. But if your entire identity centers on high performance, it is hard to even contemplate another approach to life. You just keep on climbing.

When your approach becomes more destructive than constructive, you need to find a new dimension for operating, to channel that essence of yourself. You don't try to become someone else; you become another version of yourself. I will not stop being curious, hardworking, fully engaged, and prepared. That is who I am. It is in my DNA. My new version is committed to channeling those strengths that produce positive outcomes without destroying myself in the process.

Regardless of how much planning I did for retirement, this new version of myself felt like a sudden change. The same jolt one feels when they lose their job, are laid off, or get divorced . . . Whatever happens, we are left there trying to find a new way forward. What I discovered was, at that point, I just needed to let it go. To think about the past as yesterday's news and ask what today's headlines were going to read. My retirement problem was that I wanted to continue rewriting the past. I was trying to write a different story the same way. I needed a new way to write.

My team believed that with the combination of acting on what I learned while I was a patient at the clinic and the right medication, I could experience the life I was seeking. I have to add an important caveat my team could not know: What role, if any, does potential chronic traumatic encephalopathy (CTE) contribute to my anxiety, mood swings, depression, or impulse-control problems?

CTE is caused by concussions and repeated blows to the head. Its cognitive symptoms are impaired judgment, dementia, and short-term memory loss. There was no association with CTE outside of boxing until 2002, when Dr. Bennet Omalu first discovered it during an autopsy of Pittsburgh Steelers center Mike Webster. As of today, CTE can only be confirmed by an autopsy. As of 2023, 345 of 376 deceased former NFL players whose brains were examined had CTE.

Boston University is the current center of CTE research, and over the past twelve years, I've participated in two different volunteer studies conducted there. The purpose of the research is to hopefully identify the presence of CTE in patients while they're alive and discover ways it can be treated. Significant progress has been made, but there is much more work to be done.

I've been asked if I worry about CTE and brain injury. When I do catch myself worrying about just about anything, I remember the final scene from the movie *Bridge of Spies*, starring Tom Hanks. Hanks is a CIA agent who is about to cross a bridge into Russian territory to exchange a Russian spy. Hanks looks at the spy and asks, "Are you worried?" The spy looks back and replies, "Would it make any difference?" That's how much worrying accomplishes.

As I made the fifteen-hour drive from Houston back to Asheville, I had plenty of time to contemplate what I had learned and how I could use that knowledge going forward. First and foremost in my thoughts was the fact that my psychological and emotional issues are not curable and cannot be fixed. But they had become manageable. I felt confident that I had gained a critical perspective on what was happening and acquired the tools I needed to repair the damage. I would use the same psychology I'd used with my knee rehab: I may have days where I *feel* depressed, but I will not *be* depressed. Each day would still be a good day.

When I pulled into my driveway, it was mid-March and spring had arrived. When I looked at the yard, it was with fresh eyes. Perhaps I could approach the yard not as a place to escape myself, but as a place where I could begin healing and find a new beginning. It was worth a try.

CHAPTER 17

The Garden

Once I flunked out on my initial ambitions, I gravitated back to the garden almost as a default. I needed a purpose—not a lofty goal but simply a reason for my feet to hit the ground. I needed something to apply myself to but in a new way. Growing up, I'd been pressured to always be my best. My motivation had been primarily external, which became a burden because of the constant expectations. Whether stated or unstated, they were always present. Then, I internalized that pressure.

In many ways, the garden was the ideal proof of concept for me to practice my new approach to life. For one, the metaphor for the garden was pretty much perfect. It was all about breaking new ground. Clearing some space and seeing what else wanted to grow there.

From a more pragmatic standpoint, it worked well because the stakes were low. With no one else involved, there was no one to hold me accountable, so I was free to just work. I had no timeline and no agenda beyond simply cleaning up our yard and making it look presentable. That was my sole objective.

At one and three-quarter acres, the space was big enough for me to have to really apply myself, but not so large as to be overwhelming.

The project also leveraged my strengths at the time—a strong back and a weak mind. Beyond that, it would require stamina, commitment, determination, and fortitude. The idea of doing all the work myself felt natural to me. Wielding a pickax all day long, digging out stumps and roots—that was in my programming. All I needed was the commitment to see the process through. That wouldn't be a problem. For me, having nothing to do equated to death, and I'd already determined that was not an option.

During the four years we'd lived in Asheville, I'd looked at the yard and only thought about the work involved. Sure, I could have hired someone to do it, but I figured I could do a better job myself. I knew I'd be happier with the outcome, but it was never a priority. In that time, I'd done some work in the garden, dabbling here and there, but I was mostly there to waste my time and hide from the world, including Eileen.

Coming home, I saw the garden project with fresh eyes. I wasn't hit with a lightning bolt of inspiration. I had no idea what I was going to do with the space once it was cleared, but something compelled me to believe that I could hone something positive out of it. It gave me a feeling I had not experienced in far too long. I was curious. Could I take organisms and unify them with nature to create a lasting legacy? I was hooked on finding out.

The first step was obvious. Parts of the garden looked like the forbidden forest from children's fables. Before I could get a sense of what was possible, I needed to rid the yard of its vastly overgrown tangle of unruly holly bushes, burning bushes, vines, and dead hardwoods. My days on the farm gifted me with the experience and skill set to tackle these tasks, and my

newfound disgust with our yard's appearance supplied the
necessary incentive.

To clear just half of the front yard and get it ready to
plant took the better part of a year. After months of meat-
head labor—sawing, chopping, chipping, and clearing out the
debris—I could finally start to see the canvas I was working
with. The entire yard sloped from end to end and side to side.
While this presented a challenge with erosion and drainage,
and in other respects, to me it was a worthy project. With
challenge comes opportunity. I was excited, because the elevation changes lent themselves to retaining walls and raised
beds. Hardscape is an effective way to accent nature's beauty.
Yet there was much to accomplish before I could think about
stone walls.

Once you start seeing a little bit of progress, you begin to
fantasize. To think, *I wonder if . . .* That initial curiosity and
wonderment compounded itself, and before I knew it, I was in
deep.

At that point, it was clear to me that I couldn't just sketch
out a plan for the garden and then follow it. Instead, I'd have
to learn the garden's design by doing, in much the same way
I'd learned sales. As a new sales rep at Schreiber, I'd realized
quickly that experience would be my best teacher, so I had im-
plored them to let me loose in the field. I could tell that the
garden was like that.

I function best when I'm out on the field of play. Meeting
people in person has always been my preferred way of doing
business. Actually seeing how someone acts gives me more insight than just hearing what they say. When it comes to building a team, gaining understanding, or instilling emotional
intelligence, I don't think anything can replace human interac-
tions and in-person observations. I'd have been an ineffective
leader during the pandemic, having to function with a team
that was fully remote. What all this meant for the garden was

that I couldn't just envision what I wanted; I'd need to see the materials—the plants, the stones, the fencing—and physically lay out the design. Books, websites, and catalogs would be of no use to me.

As it turned out, clearing the aboveground foliage and debris was nothing compared to the labor that awaited me underground. Stones, roots, ivy, old drains, and beer bottles all had to be removed, and not just torn out from the surface but to a depth of sixteen to twenty inches, so plant roots had healthy soil in which to grow. I spent many days with dirty hands that I proudly displayed as my red badge of courage. The sheer intensity of my labor required that I pace myself, and that afforded me the time necessary to adjust to a life without goals or competition. Instead of focusing on always doing more or working harder—achieving more results—I hacked and dug away, letting my mind wander to the endless possibilities that stretched before me. As tedious and exhausting as the work was, I accepted everything in order to keep moving. There were mornings that when I rose and laced up my boots, they were still warm from the day before.

I have always been intrigued by how some great artists and composers can go days without sleeping and eating. The garden gave me a similar experience, perhaps to a lesser degree. I imagine that the artists' passion for their work and the euphoria of creating something that had only been in their mind drove them to such extraordinary measures. In other words, they experienced passion, and they did that by doing the work. They did not go out and find passion, as we are so often instructed to do.

I believe that passion is not a virtue or a goal. It is not a present, sitting there waiting to be opened. You need to get in there and unwrap it. Passion is a result, not a goal. It is not a panacea for lacking motivation, feeling unfulfilled, finding purpose, or just about anything else that can contribute to falling short of your life's ambitions. Passion is a pull, not a push. It's not a plant you can yell at and expect to bloom. It evolves and develops over time, in the course of action. Football had been the first passion I'd developed, and now it's my garden.

Some people go through life without even having one passion, and in spite of what self-help books and blogs of today tell you, that's not a bad thing. I know plenty of people who admit to not having had a driving passion, and they're very happy with their lives. That might not be the case had they spent their lives looking for something they could never find or judging their lack of passion. As the saying goes, if it ain't broke . . .

Typically, when people think about passion, they think about what the return's going to be, imagining something tangible. Often, that amounts to getting paid for it, and sometimes that works out. But these days, I get equally as satisfied from digging a hole as I used to from hitting a sales goal. I know that into that hole will go a plant or a tree or some flowers that I'll get to enjoy later. If you don't enjoy the process as much as the end product, then you're pursuing the wrong things. That's why so many of us can't get ourselves to do those shit jobs. We don't see the value or return over time; we only look at the return in time.

My garden project was briefly interrupted when I received a call from a small volunteer group seeking my help. They'd received a grant to install a learning garden at a local elementary school and wanted assistance.

Over the period of six weeks, we transformed a plot of land about the size of half a football field. When we finished, it was covered in raised plant beds filled with vegetables, flowers, blueberry shrubs, and a water garden.

Aside from the delight I experienced at finally being able to contribute effectively to an effort that helped others, I also received an unexpected reward. Through this work, I was introduced to a variety of plants, materials, and suppliers that I knew would be helpful for my own project. The relationships I developed with my suppliers were invaluable to the success of the garden. They helped me understand the role plant texture, configuration, shape, and size play in the overall effect of an area. Prior to this education, my understanding of plants had been limited to knowing which end to place in the ground.

As I began touring the local nurseries, I realized that the most important plant criteria, at least for my purposes, was maturity. I wasn't interested in creating a garden that would take twenty years to mature. I wanted instant gratification. It would be of little use to me to imagine my grandchildren one day saying, "I wish Papa were alive to see this."

Some of the plants I was working with had root balls that were five feet in diameter and four feet deep. They weighed as much as twenty-five hundred pounds. The only piece of equipment I had was a wheelbarrow. Determined to continue with my plan of doing all the work myself, I went out and bought a twenty-three-horsepower Bobcat tractor with a forty-eight-inch bucket. I would need a bigger piece of equipment to handle plants weighing more than a thousand pounds, but the Bobcat would be a valuable addition to my arsenal. I also located a 2001 Dodge Ram 2500 pickup truck with a dump bed. I was now in complete control of purchasing, installation, logistics, and design. I was a one-man band, and I could play any song I wanted. The only thing missing was the tune—a vision.

Prior to entering treatment, I thought of a garden as a place to grow flowering plants for indoor and outdoor use. Maybe I would plant hollyhocks like the ones my grandmother planted along the chicken coop, morning glories like my mother planted that climbed the lamppost in the front yard, or wildflowers like the ones that grew in the pasture fields. But these thoughts changed.

During my exit interview at the clinic, my therapist shared with me his findings. I'd spent my entire life living for what comes next—the next achievement, the next challenge, the next something. It was about trying to get people to love me for what I've done, rather than just loving myself for who I am.

The garden has helped me stay focused on the present and myself, but so has Mother Nature. She reminds me every day that the past and the future are not relevant, only today. My time in the garden has taught me how to focus on each day and not be consumed with yesterday or tomorrow, because I cannot do anything about either. Creating a garden for the purpose of visual appeal is affected by the weather conditions of yesterdays and tomorrows, but all I can do is adjust. Temperature, wind, and moisture are all conditions that impact the look of a garden, none of which I can control.

That's a profound lesson the garden has taught me. That in life, I cannot control what happens to me. What people say, what people do, and what unforeseen events and changes occur are all out of my control. The only thing I can control is how I react and respond to the present. Nothing is done to you; we do it to ourselves.

When I was beaten like a drum during my first game playing for Ohio State, my coach pointed out to me that my failings were not the result of anything my opponent did to me but what I did to myself. When I find myself dealing with poor outcomes, I focus on what I did to contribute to the situation.

My challenge now was to create a vision relying on other sensory components beyond just the visual. A place that stimulated my emotions, feelings, and sense of being. I had absolutely no idea how to create such a garden, but I knew that I would recognize it when it happened. So instead of being guided by drawings, pictures, or plans, I let my instincts, observations, and emotions dictate my decisions. My litmus test for every one of the plant beds was: When I look at it, does it wrap its arms around me and give me a big hug? I wasn't interested in *Wow!* I was more interested in a sense of *I can't believe how this makes me feel* or *I love where this takes my thoughts and my mind.*

No detail was too small. Nothing was inconsequential. I considered everything with great care, from the curvature and size of the beds, the shape and color of the stones used in the retaining walls and the water feature, the gravel for the walkways, and the color and texture of the mulch. Extraordinary results can only be achieved by attending to every detail. At the most competitive levels, paying attention to details is the difference between winning and losing, good and great, success and failure. You will not have done your best without attending to the small stuff.

The theme I landed on is that all thirty beds in the garden are planted with at least one "star" as part of its design. It could be a fifty-year-old Viridis Japanese maple with a stunning canopy, a forty-foot weeping fir, or a European white pine. Accompanying each star is a supporting cast that showcases and accentuates the main feature and its surrounding area. The beds are raised to offer a stage for my stars.

I built the Invaders in much the same way. I complemented our featured running back with quick and agile offensive linemen. Our wide receivers ran precise routes to take advantage of our quarterbacks' accuracy. Defensively, our schemes were blitzing and stunting, while utilizing our linemen's ability to change direction and confuse the opponent. I put plants and players in the prime position to do their best.

The beauty with nature is that you can put on different shows at the same time. In one bed, it might be gauras waving in unison in the breeze, another bed is Shasta daisies smiling for the photographers, and another is a Korean fir with its white tips pretending it's Christmas. No matter where you are in the garden, it is showtime. Over time, the garden was becoming a showplace, not a showpiece.

Seven years after starting the garden, Eileen and I decided to host a garden tour to raise money for a local nonprofit. On a sunny afternoon, more than 150 guests attended. It was the first chance I had to validate my suspicions. I was delighted to hear our guests use words such as *moving, calm, thrilling,* and *breathtaking.* Some were too emotional to describe their impressions.

By the end of the third hour, the porch and the decks were empty, but our guests hadn't left. Everyone was in the garden, spread out and sitting on benches, walls, steps, or blankets on the grass. I heard one guest ask a server if they could bring them some refreshments, "because I don't want to lose my spot." I knew then that I was well on my way to realizing my vision. Had I known this was how our guests were feeling, I would have played through the gardens' speakers Norman Greenbaum's 1969 hit song, "Spirit in the Sky."

A garden created from a vision rather than a plan is realized only by recognition. I knew if something worked or if it didn't once I saw it. This process of trial and error is steeped in change. Everything is subject to relocation. Nearly 30 percent of the over twenty-five hundred plants in the garden have been relocated. Some as many as four or five times. I have become very good at digging holes.

This approach accounts for why it's taken more than twelve years and twenty-four thousand hours for the garden to reach the "stage" it's in today.

It was the same transformation I made my senior year at OSU. I was a good offensive tackle at 265 pounds, but I became an All-American by getting 38 pounds lighter. As one renowned global design firm motto puts it, "Fail often to succeed sooner." I was willing to give up the good for the great.

The backyard was not without its challenges, the first of which was removing a one-hundred-by-fifty-foot koi pond. The previous owner was very proud of what he had built, but to me it was a breeding ground for mosquitos, and it was positioned directly in the middle of the yard. After the water was pumped out and the three remaining koi were relocated, the hole was backfilled, and I set aside the boulders used to hold the back wall for later use.

One set of the bedroom doors to the back of the house overlooks a fifteen-foot drop that extends about twenty feet. I decided to install a water feature on the side of that hill. After two days of digging out the basin so the water would form a pool, I encountered a buried tree stump three feet in diameter. It took another two days to remove the stump and its connected roots. Once the site was cleared, it took a week to lay the piping and electrical wiring, position the liner, and configure the boulders, many of which came from the koi pond.

Building a water feature was similar to the experience with the startup I was involved in. After all the work is completed, you have no idea if it will function as it is intended until it is launched. I am certain Thomas Edison felt the same way when he flipped the switch to the electric lightbulb. Fortunately, my first attempt at the water feature was a success, unlike the startup, which went up in flames.

I wanted my water feature to produce the same sounds as a mountain stream. Most water features sound like water running from a faucet, a steady stream that sounds monotone. Mountain streams have a deep baritone and bass. A friend told me the water sounds from mountains are produced when water flows over, around, and between the stones covering the borders and the beds of the stream, creating an echo effect. Armed with this information, I placed a water valve in a cavity built into the head of the falls. Water runs into the cavity, creating an echo, and then flows out of a slight opening in the face of the cavity. If Leonard Cohen and Barry White sung a duet, their voices would produce sounds similar to my waterfalls.

As much as I learned about creating the sights and sounds of a water feature, I became aware of something more useful. Before my friend responded to my request for information about streams, he wanted to know exactly what I was trying to accomplish. Once he had gathered as much information as he needed, he responded. I then realized the difference between advice and opinion. Advice is experience applied to information. The more information and experience someone has, the more valuable their information becomes. When you are receiving advice, take notes. When it's an opinion someone offers you, run!

Over time, I expanded the garden's personality beyond plant material and hardscape. This included reclaiming five horse-stall doors from a farm in Lexington, Kentucky, and incorporating them throughout the garden. I also added a steel statue from a local artist, a piece called *Prayer to the Universe*, that greets visitors entering the front walkway. In addition to the sculpture's unique design is its surface. There are no welds or markings. The artist achieved this look by cutting the design from a single sheet of steel. The process took two people more than two months to complete.

My intention for the garden was to create a place that speaks to the present, but over time, I found it had other voices. I designed features into the landscape that reminded me of those people who made me a better person during our time together.

My mother's only sibling was married to a woman with the most infectious smile. I planted several beds of a rose variety called Drift that remind me of her.

Outside our bedroom window is a fringe tree that blooms in April, the same month my youngest brother took his life.

My friend who reintroduced me to the Indiana cheerleader back in the day died from Parkinson's disease. In his honor, I planted a rare Japanese maple. His wife died a few years later. When I visited her before her passing, we would often speak about the lavender gardens in France. Before she died, I was able to show her a picture of the seventy-five lavender plantings in "Emmy's Bed."

My best friend and teammate, Tom DeLeone, who played offensive center next to me for the Browns and the Buckeyes, died from brain cancer. He was also later diagnosed with stage-four CTE. In his memory is planted a paperbark Japanese maple. The most captivating feature of this tree is its bark. As the name implies, the bark is paper thin, and when the sun shines on it, the illumination is so bright that it appears to be on fire. That was Tom, a fiery personality with a fierce love for his friends, teammates, family, and convictions.

For my dear friends and neighbors in Cleveland who chaperoned the boys from Cleveland to San Francisco and stayed with us for two weeks until we got situated, there is a metal sculpture of concentric shapes that intertwine into one piece. It represents how tightly their lives were connected, as though they were Romeo and Juliet. I designed a water garden bed with their sculpture as the focal point.

Not long ago, I was in a local jewelry store looking for a birthday gift for Eileen. In the estate-section display case was a pocket watch very similar to the one my grandfather, Art, wore to church on Sundays with his three-piece suit. The watch was called a repeater because it chimed on the hour, half hour, and quarter hour. It was popular before the invention of electricity, because you could tell time in the dark by the sound and the number of times it chimed. This watch was made in England, ironically the same year Grandpa was born, 1890. Art's memory is in the garden, not as a plant but in the watch that resides in the watch pocket of my work jeans.

I saved a small plot of ground to use as a learning garden for my grandchildren to serve the same purpose as the garden we planted for the elementary school. Each time they visit from Green Bay, Wisconsin, we undertake new projects. We visit nurseries for new plants, care for the existing plants by pruning and fertilizing, and clean the beds. Each grandchild has a task for which they are responsible. They do not need to grow up on a farm to learn what it means to do the work and get your hands dirty.

Along the walkway to our front door, driven into the ground, is a tribute to my English Labrador, Bucky. Hanging from the top of the stake is a one-gallon green plastic water pitcher punctured with holes. The pitcher is attached by Bucky's dog collar. He was eight weeks old when I started working in the garden and was by my side every day. He would toss his pitcher into the air and catch it, retrieve it when I threw it, or clench it in his teeth and shake it back and forth. Everywhere I went in the truck, he was in the shotgun seat, playing his best Jessica Tandy imitation in *Driving Miss Daisy*, and I was Morgan Freeman. He was the most wonderful companion I could have ever wished for.

Soon after Bucky turned eight years old, his behavior shifted. Something just wasn't right. I took him to the vet, and he was diagnosed with Lyme disease. After eight days of treatment at a veterinary hospital, he did not respond, so I brought him home. From my days on the farm, I knew the look in an animal's eyes when they were suffering, so I made the heartbreaking decision to let Bucky go. It was one of the saddest days of my life. The pitcher is in his memory. Some of his ashes are scattered around his favorite resting area, and the remainder of his ashes will join me in different sites of the yard when that time comes.

As with most things we value in life, we want to protect them. The garden was becoming one of those things, so I hired a company to build an eight-foot fence around the property. I had dug enough postholes and strung enough wire fencing on the farm that I decided to afford myself this one luxury. It has prevented deer from eating my perennials as if they were cabbage, rabbits from eating every flower petal they could reach, and bucks from rubbing their antlers against the bark of my Japanese maples.

The fence has kept out the critters but has not kept out the dangers from within, namely voles, moles, mites, fungi, and deer ticks. As for the internal thieves that steal my plants in the night, I have discovered remedies that either rid or control such invasions.

At least I did not revert to a tactic used by one of my friends. He bought a miniature pinscher to rid his property of moles and voles. The dog was unsuccessful, and he was left with a yard that looked like Bill Murray's groundskeeper character from *Caddyshack* had visited.

Much like with the garden, I have learned that harm from within the barriers we build can also be damaging. I was always concerned with who my sons associated with at school, their use of the internet, and their safety. Those were all outside disruptors beyond my protective barriers. What I should have been concerned about was the discord and negative influences created inside our home: divorce, addiction, and insecurity.

The biggest failings in my life have been self-inflicted, and all of them could have been avoided. Beware the dangers that lurk within, for they pose the greatest threat.

In the spring of 2022, I was approached by three members of a garden club in Asheville. Two of them had attended our open house and fundraiser a few years earlier. They thought the garden was worthy of recommendation into the Smithsonian Institution's Archives of American Gardens (AAG) series. I had no clue such an organization existed, but I was interested, until I learned about the application process. Among the elements required were digital pictures taken from the same location at different times of the year, a site map of every plant along with their Latin and common names, a design of the garden to scale, and a list of features that make the garden unique. Completing such an application was far above my pay grade. Assigning the Latin and common names to over 360 varieties of plants alone would have taken me an eternity.

My anxieties were relieved when the trio informed me that they would complete the application; I only needed to provide a name for the garden. By the fall of 2023, the application was ready for submission, but I had not settled on a name. That is until one morning, when I received a text from Tyler that read simply "Bucky's Run." Neither the garden nor Bucky could have received a better tribute.

On February 7, 2024, Bucky's Run became one of the sixty-five hundred members of the AAG.

I have been asked by Eileen and others what I plan to do "now that the garden is complete." The garden will never be done, only closer than when I started. I did think I was finished with the intensive work, but Mother Nature had other ideas.

On Eileen's birthday, September 27, 2024, Hurricane Helene stormed through the Carolinas, bringing with it the worst devastation in the state's history. One hundred and seven people were killed, forty-three of whom lived in my county. The damage for the state is expected to be more than $53 billion.

Fallen trees made the roads and even walkways impassable. I couldn't see out the windows, much less leave the house. City water lines erupted, power lines were down, and there was no internet or cable. Connection with your neighbor, much less the outside world, was nonexistent. The closest open banks, grocery stores, gas stations, and retail stores were fifty miles away. Cleanup was interrupted in the first week because of a shortage of diesel fuel needed to power equipment. Our neighbor had more than two hundred trees blow over on their four acres of property. As I looked at the destruction, I could not find the words to describe it.

The more difficult a situation is, the more you learn about yourself and those around you. There were neighbors who joined me in putting all our energy into the present and figuring out what we could do to mitigate our situation. There were others who could only lament what they had lost and worry about tomorrow. It was wasted energy. By focusing on what we could control, we made progress in our cleanup efforts and restored calm and a sense of normalcy.

Fortunately, the garden fared well, relatively speaking. Four large oak trees in the front yard were uprooted, the largest of which had a root ball of over ten feet in diameter and had to be removed with a crane. I viewed the destruction caused by these fallen trees as an opportunity to make the area better than it was before the storm.

The efforts I thought were in my rearview mirror had reappeared. It took three months to replant the three damaged beds and find new stars to put on a different show. One of the stars I found was a rare Japanese maple that was grown in a nursery outside Portland, Oregon. It was planted as a seedling by the original owner more than fifty-five years ago and was harvested by his grandson. The storm made that possible.

The garden project was initially driven by curiosity, hope, and the need for change, but evolved into a thing of wonder, deep emotion, and fulfillment. As I gaze upon the garden now, I am amazed every day not by what I see but by what it offers and represents.

The garden reminds me that without experiencing adversity, failure, or setbacks or doing the work, I would not have realized the quiet, satisfaction, and contentment I now feel in my soul when I am in the garden's presence. Hallelujah!

Epilogue

Writing a book about your life is a curious endeavor. It's different from simply reflecting on your experience, though it certainly involves a lot of that. I've had to learn how to view my life as a story—to create a narrative and identify themes. And I can tell you that the main theme is this: Do the work.

Every positive outcome I have experienced was the result of my willingness to actively engage with my circumstances, using the resources available to me at the time. Certainly, factors such as luck, timing, and state of mind all played a role at times, but if I hadn't been willing to do the work, none of it would have mattered.

I'm reminded of a TV series that was popular when I was growing up, *The Many Loves of Dobie Gillis*. In the show, the character Maynard G. Krebs, who was played by Bob Denver, had an extreme aversion to work. So much so that when he merely heard the word, he would go into a panic. "Work!" he'd scream. Yes, Maynard, work. Somehow, we got this idea that work is antithetical to pleasure, but I think they collaborate, together creating that sense of satisfaction I have learned to relish.

It's not about simply pushing as hard as you can. It's about being willing to deeply and continuously examine everything in your life that's under your control, and trying to improve it. That doesn't mean you're not *good enough* as is. We all have inherent worth. But the thing is, we also have sensitive bullshit meters, whether we're aware of it or not. Deep down, you're not going to *feel* worthy if you're just trying to skate through life doing as little as possible or, even worse, if you're trying to blame all your circumstances or outcomes on externals.

At the outset of this journey, I mentioned that as I considered my life, I realized it followed a blueprint. To paraphrase Steve Jobs in his famous Stanford commencement speech, I looked back and connected the dots. When I did that, I discovered that in many ways, this book and my life were guided by three *Cs . . .*

Curiosity pushed me to wonder, over and over again, "Can I do this?" It could be a task as simple as digging a hole or as risky as changing careers midlife. Consistently, it was the pull of the unknown that drove my decisions.

Confidence gave me the courage to overcome any doubts, setbacks, failures, and adversity—and there were plenty of all of them—that I faced in life. From a career-ending injury to being forced to seek mental-health care, I didn't always know how I could prevail, but I knew that I would.

And *conviction* provided me with the determination to never quit. I was willing to do the work, leave no doubts, and make the sacrifices necessary to always achieve my best. Conviction stands above all else. Being curious and confident alone will not culminate in your best without conviction.

In life, we're influenced by factors outside our control, but the fact is that we have far more ability to shape our outcomes than we realize. I promise you that if you learn to engage with and maximize your internals, that doesn't mean you'll have a perfect life—I certainly haven't—but you'll quickly lose your appetite for lethargy or blame. Once you see the massive impact that doing the work has on your life and your outlook, more likely than not, you'll be hooked. Just as I've been.

These days, when I look out across the garden, it's not to

assess what needs to change. Instead, it's more about manicuring. In the garden as with my life, the hay is in the barn. The bulk of the labor is complete, and my focus now is on maintaining what I've worked hard to create so that I can share it with others.

Acknowledgments

FRIENDS (MORE LIKE FAMILY)

To the Swanson Family (Cleveland, Ohio), the Meuser Family (Moraga, California), the Wilson Family (Oakville, Ontario), Howard and Rita Friedman (Lake Tahoe, California), Tony and Molly Gartner (Hilton Head, South Carolina), Marci and Dave Schroeder (Asheville, North Carolina), and Roger and Pam Schreiber (Grand Coulee, Washington):

Thank you for your love and support, and for always being there for me and my family.

MENTORS

To my grandfather, Art Wadsworth; my mom and dad, Archie and Mary Anna Hutchison; Tim Opel (retired president) and Larry Ferguson (retired CEO) of Schreiber Foods; Coach John Ralston; Coach Forrest Gregg; Coach Woody Hayes; and Coach Hugh Hindman:

Your trust and confidence in me helped me reach my full potential.

BOOK CONTRIBUTORS

To Nic and Thad Davis, Emily Glaser, John Boneparth, Gail

Harris, Linda and Marque Gritta, Logan Fischer, Patrick Rini, and Rusty Wilson:

Your honest feedback and suggestions steered me throughout the writing of *Getting My Hands Dirty*.

To Henk Rivers (Charleston, South Carolina):

Your encouragement and faith gave me the courage to write my first sentence.

SPECIAL THANKS AND RECOGNITION

To my editor, Kelly Madrone, whose talent, support, and guidance brought this project to light and gave it life. I am forever grateful.

"A life well lived cannot be lived alone."
—Chuck Hutchison, April 2025

About the Author

CHUCK HUTCHISON grew up in rural Ohio and was a member of The Ohio State University's 1968 National Championship football team. His success in football took him to the NFL, where he played for seven seasons. A seeker of possibilities—both inside and outside of the game—Hutchison also formed a start-up football franchise, became a contract negotiator for the Green Bay Packers, and worked as a sales executive for one of the top one hundred privately-held companies in the US. Retirement offered him the opportunity to create a garden that was accepted into the Smithsonian's Archives of American Gardens. Hutchison lives and gardens in Asheville, North Carolina.